Annette Funicello

Tributes from Fans and Friends

Rita Rose

Theme Park Press
The Happiest Books on Earth
www.ThemeParkPress.com

Theme Park Press is not associated with the Walt Disney Company.

The views expressed in this book are those of the author and do not necessarily reflect the views of Theme Park Press.

Theme Park Press publishes its books in a variety of print and electronic formats. Some content that appears in one format may not appear in another.

Editor: Bob McLain
Layout: Artisanal Text
Cover photo and design: Nick Strange
Mouseketeer photo © The Walt Disney Company

ISBN 978-1-68390-253-9
Printed in the United States of America

Theme Park Press | www.ThemeParkPress.com
Address queries to bob@themeparkpress.com

Contents

"Annette Funicello was effortlessly genuine."

—David Stollery

Introduction

Nothing bad was ever supposed to happen to Annette Funicello. She led a charmed life. She was kind, unpretentious and pretty, and lacked ego in a profession that practically demands it. She was our sweet, shy Mouseketeer and our young, beautiful beach girl. So when Annette announced to the world in 1992 that she had Multiple Sclerosis, we lost a big chunk of our innocence. How could Annette be sick? We were devastated by the unfairness of her diagnosis.

I'll never forget the afternoon that I got a phone call from Annette, just a couple of days before the initial announcement of her MS that first appeared in *USA Today*. She started out with the usual chit-chat, then she said, "I have something to tell you, and I want you to hear it from me before it appears in the newspaper." I didn't know anything about MS, and she explained it was a disease of the central nervous system, and hers was progressive. I don't remember my response, I was so stunned. She was five years into her diagnosis before revealing it to the public: Only her second husband, Glen Holt, her mother and three kids knew. Later, she said she was afraid of hurting her fans, or that people wouldn't love her anymore if she revealed her disease.

"I didn't go public for a long time because I believed people wanted to think that nothing bad ever happens to Annette," she said.

She couldn't have been more wrong about her fans, or anyone else in her life. Everyone rallied around and supported her.

I was in high school when I started my Annette Funicello National Fan Club. There were several other clubs for her in the 1960s, and we presidents got to know each other and enjoyed sharing photos and information on our favorite star.

Many of us are still friends today, and we're in our 70s! My club continued for nearly three decades, during which time I was immersed in the fandom that surrounded Annette. Her participation was more than I ever expected—she always gave 100 percent to everything she did. She provided autographed pictures, wrote letters, answered questions from fans and kept me up-to-date on the latest news. She sent wonderful gifts and beautiful handwritten letters.

I started out as a fan and became a friend. Her friends call her Annie, she said, so I called her Annie too. When she invited me and another fan club president, Bonnie Kirn Wendt, to her wedding to Jack Gilardi in 1965, we were surprised—and thrilled! And, of course, we went to California to share her special day. The first time I met Annette, she was wearing a wedding dress.

When the Internet became popular in the mid-'90s, several groups dedicated to Annette, including our fan club, popped up on Yahoo. Then we moved over to Facebook, where there currently are a half dozen fan pages dedicated to Annette. Instagram and other social media also have Annette pages. Facebook was hugely instrumental in connecting me to fans as well as several people interviewed for this book.

When Annette passed away on April 8, 2013, she had lived with MS for 26 years. And while we mourned her death, I also wondered what would happen to those of us who had been dedicated fans since the *Mickey Mouse Club*. What happened was, we never lost our admiration for Annette. Every day I log onto Facebook and see photos and other posts about her with enthusiastic responses from hundreds of fans. We are still here, and we will never stop loving Annette Funicello.

One thing that I've discovered over the years, after interacting with fans from all over the USA and Canada, is that if you know someone is an admirer of Annette's, you already know a lot about that person. Annette had a great appreciation for her fans and became friends with many of them. Fans are the backbone of any celebrity's success. Without them, celebrity quickly fades.

And so, this book is dedicated to all of her fans.

Most of us know the stories behind Annette's relationships with other celebrities, but this book digs a little deeper. I found people who knew Annette for a few minutes, a few weeks or several years, all of whom were impacted by their encounters with her. Her bestie, actress Shelley Fabares, talks about how Annette became her lifetime friend and confidante. But most of the others are people you've probably never heard of, whose stories and photos will be new to you. Sandy Ferra, a childhood friend, relives the years before Annette became famous. Kevin Kidney relates his story about designing Annette's famous Disney cane, and how he eventually got to meet her. A late-in-life friend, Kathy Maraldo, recounts the many trips Annette made to New Orleans and how she was able to help Annette after her MS diagnosis.

In this book are pictures of Annette with nearly everyone I interviewed, plus rare family photos that were given to Nick Strange, a fan and family friend, to archive. His story is here, too. These memories of Annette take on different forms: Some friends wrote their own, some preferred to be interviewed, and some told me their stories that I made into narratives. They all give insight into Annette's impeccable character.

Annette's mom, Virginia Funicello, passed away in 2007, but she is represented here, too. Virgie was very much involved with Annette's fans. She often invited them to the Funicello home when Annette was young, and always enjoyed a phone call from fan/friends as Annette's career progressed. When she showed up for Annette's events she consistently made a point of interacting with those who attended. Virgie was a fun, chatty redhead who had endless stories to tell and food to offer. Included in this book is her story, reprinted from a fan club journal (fanzine).

Annette was always family-oriented and had no problem scaling back her career to raise the three Gilardi children, Gina, Jacky and Jason. She was an engaged mom who drove car pools and worked at the Little League snack bar. It is heartbreaking to know that she is unable to enjoy being in the lives of her children and her four beautiful grandchildren.

I hope you'll enjoy the reminiscences in this book and feel the enduring affection from those who shared their Annette stories. Somewhere, her bright Mouseke-light is shining down on all of us.

—Rita Rose

Shelley Fabares

Best Friend

Anyone who has followed Annette's career—and life—knows that Shelley Fabares was her BFF. They met in catechism class then worked together on the Mickey Mouse Club's "Annette" series, where their friendship blossomed. As best friends, Annette and Shelley spent a lot of time together, trying to lead a normal life outside of Hollywood. It was a solid, 57-year friendship that saw them through many life events.

Shelley became an actress at age three, then went on to star in several TV series, most notably The Donna Reed Show and Coach, three Elvis movies, the TV movie Brian's Song and many others. In 1962, her recording of "Johnny Angel" reached Number One on the Billboard Hot 100 chart. Here is Shelley's story:

Like everybody else in the '50s, I watched the *Mickey Mouse Club* every day. My favorite Mouseketeer was Annette: I just loved her, and when she was on the screen I went crazy. She was so darling and sweet and beautiful. And when it was time for me to make my confirmation in the Catholic Church, there was a big surprise in store for me!

I had left Blessed Sacrament Catholic School, where Mouseketeer Doreen Tracey had been a classmate and friend, to go to public school. Then, at my first Catechism class in eighth grade, the door opened and in walked Doreen...with Annette! It was like the top of my head blew off! Annette was phenomenally popular and everybody loved her. Doreen introduced me to her, but we were both very shy. We didn't talk a lot, but I loved going to Catechism class to see Annette once a week.

Two or three months after our confirmation, I went to Disney Studios for an interview, but I didn't know what it was for. Then my agent called and told my mom I got the part in something called the "Annette" serial on the *Mickey Mouse Club*. When Mom got off the phone and told me, I almost fainted. When I read the script, I was so excited to be in it, even though I played a mean town girl who was nasty to Annette. I had to pinch myself every day working with her!

It was while we were filming "Annette" that our friendship took off. There was a scene where a bunch of kids were going on a hayride and the director told everyone to get into the wagon. Well, everybody jumped on and immediately got into couples. Annette and I were the last two on, so we sat in the front. Everyone behind us was laughing and flirting. We started laughing about how the other couples were flirting and we didn't have anybody to flirt with...and that was the beginning of our friendship!

From then on, we found out all those things we had in common, like being brought up in strict Catholic families and working at a young age. She had other friends but they were mostly Mouseketeers. I felt like I had known her forever—we just clicked. I spent so much time at her house that I became the Funicellos' other daughter. They called me Shelley Fabrocini, haha.

I'll never forget one time when Annette and her mom, Virginia, had some fun with my shyness. Annette and I had a friend, Sandy Ferra, whose parents were friends with the Funicellos, so we would sometimes hang out together. *(See Sandy Ferra Martindale's story elsewhere in this book.)* Sandy's dad owned several nightclubs, and one New Year's Eve they invited Annette's family to party at a club called The Crossbow. They asked me to come along with them, but I didn't want to go where I wasn't invited. Virginia said, "Come on, it'll be all right." When we got there, I hesitated getting out of the car. Annette was laughing at me and Virginia asked if I was all right. I said I guessed so, even though I felt queasy. Then Virginia said, "Just don't throw up on anybody." Annette and I broke up laughing, although I was mortified. But I didn't get sick!

Annette and I flourished and grew in many of the same ways. We would go to Mass together, we liked some of the same boys...we did everything together. I felt like I was meeting the other half of me. We understood one another and had a remarkable friendship for so many years. When you're really best friends, no one else exists in the world.

Some of my favorite times together seem to center on laughing. We laughed at everything we found funny. We laughed all the time, every weekend when we spent the night at each other's places. We gossiped, we laughed, we ate, we talked about boys and clothes, all the things teens do most of the time. If it hadn't been for my friendship with Annette I wouldn't have had those normal experiences. I had other friends, but when I was working they were in school, so with Annette it was entirely different. We worked at different studios but had some of the same experiences.

It was an incredible era for us to be in. And we were the "good girls." Disney wanted Annette to be good and virginal, and not wear a bikini. After *Donna Reed*, I was almost always cast as the nice, sweet girl in movies.

It's always hard to talk about someone you love so much and make it sound like a true reflection of what that person is like. I owe so much of my ability to love others to my wonderful relationship with Annette. It was remarkable just being together. Show business is entirely different now ... we had no social media and no connections to meet up with people out in the world.

Of course our friendship changed once we became adults and got married. I never had kids but Annette had three, and once babies come into your life your relationship takes a new direction. But amazingly, we stayed as close as we ever had been. Annette was totally devoted to her kids, but that didn't get in the way of our friendship or the quality of our time together. I'd go to her house and we'd laugh, have a glass of wine, and talk about old times and new times. Annette was very much a homebody and her first husband, Jack, was an outgoing talent agent with a lot of professional events to go to. Annette was happier at home with the kids and making dinner.

She did several beach movies and I did three with Elvis. She and I always felt the same way about how the ocean air played havoc with our hair! Our naturally curly hair was the bane of our existence. Fans would see our photos in movie magazines and write about wanting to do their hair just like us! Our relationship allowed Annette and me to have the same experiences regular kids had while living an unusual life. I know I would have missed that without Annette.

When I found out she had MS, I was devastated, and that doesn't really describe it. I didn't have a real clear understanding of MS but I saw the problems she was having. I couldn't believe it—it was like the other half of me was disappearing. It was horrifying to see what was happening to her. Early on, some doctors said they didn't know what she had but that it wasn't MS. This gave Annette and Glen, her second husband, tremendous hope. But she kept getting worse and finally it was definitely diagnosed. For me, it continues to be devastating to this day.

After their house fire in 2011, Glen moved Annette to Bakersfield, where he had lived before they got married. I was doing *Coach* and my second marriage, to Mike Farrell, brought a new life with two stepchildren. Still, I went to see her whenever I could.

My mother passed away from Alzheimer's. With that disease, the patient withdraws and becomes a shell of their former self. In some ways MS has the same effect. It was very hard to visit with Annette, hard to communicate. At a certain point conversations with her became totally one-sided. It broke my heart. It was an awful period of time because Annette's friendship was so much a part of me.

I was with Annette when she died. She was in the hospital with pneumonia when Glen called me to come up to see her. I got to the hospital two days before she passed away. She was finally in a large room with family members as well as Sharon Baird, her close Mouseketeer friend. Glen came in to talk to us when it became clear Annette was leaving us.

We each went up to her bed and talked to her for a moment. I believe she could hear us, and I'd like to think she knew we were there. I whispered a couple of funny things to her and told her how much I loved her. Then we sat down, and none of us could talk—we didn't know what to say. I watched the heart monitor; she plateaued for a while, but then the numbers started going down fast, and then she was gone. She was finally free.

There were many facets to Annette's personality. She was kind, funny, caring, lovely inside and out—plus so much more than most people knew. And she was brave, because she withstood so much. I am enormously grateful to God that I got to be with her for all of those special, laughter-filled years."

Shelley Fabares and
Annette were best
friends for 57 years.
(Photo: American
International Pictures)

Shelley and Annette spent hours together as
teenagers, talking about clothes and boys.

Nick Strange

New York Fan

Sometimes you don't know where a connection to Annette will lead you.

For Nick Strange, a fan from Oneida, New York, meeting Annette led to becoming a member of her family. He didn't have to marry anyone: He only had to be a handsome Italian guy with a flair for photography and a fondness for the elder Funicellos and Albanos, who lived close to him in Utica, Annette's hometown in upstate New York.

It started when Nick, a longtime member of my Annette Fan Club, was working the photo shop for the club after Lou Fitton took over. As a Flatware Designer Craftsman for Oneida Ltd., he heard that Annette liked Oneida silverware products, so he sent her a letter and several brochures.

"I had just gotten back from teaching an exercise class when my phone rang and I heard a voice say, 'Hi, this is Annette. I got your brochures and wondered if you could order something for me for (Mouseketeer) Sharon's mother.' She told me what to order," Nick recalls, "and I said I'd let her know if it was available. I called her the next night and told her the item could be shipped from the factory to her. She thanked me and said she had heard good things about me. What a compliment!

"Well, after that I got a call from her Aunt Mickie in Utica, asking me if I could order a particular flatware pattern that Virginia wanted; I said I could do that. Then Mickie and another sister, Carmella, met me at the store to pick up the order. A few days later, they called and invited me for dinner with all three of Virginia's sisters. That was how it all started."

Annette's aunts Mickie (Michelina) and Jo (Josephine, Annette's godmother), neither of whom had children, easily adopted Nick into the family. Carmella and Frank "Windy" Barletto welcomed him, too. Soon he was calling them aunt and uncle.

"Annette's family wanted me for holidays, birthdays and other occasions, but that made it hard sometimes because I had my own family celebrations," says Nick. "Uncle Windy would invite me over for dinner and then we'd go hang out in the garage. I also invited them to my house for meals. If I invited one aunt to the house, they'd all come. It was a package deal.

"Uncle Windy worked in an Italian bakery in early morning where he sliced Italian bread. Sometimes there was enough dough left over to make humongous rolls, 12 inches in diameter. He would slice the rolls and put cold cuts and cheese in them to make us huge sandwiches. He also was friends with people who owned a produce business. One day, as I got home from work, I found Uncle Windy, Aunt Car and Aunt Mickie sitting on my front porch waiting for me. Uncle Windy had brought me a huge box of bananas, tomatoes, peppers and onions. He said, 'You're gonna eat these, aren't you?' There was no way I could eat everything so I gave some away to friends.

"They just took hold of me. And if I didn't call them every other day, Uncle Windy would call me and say, 'You forgot the old man!' I can hear him now. I was a fan of Annette's, but they treated me like family. Our conversations weren't always about Annette, but they'd tell me stories about when she was young."

Nick didn't meet Annette in person until 1989, although he had talked to her by phone several times.

"She'd tell me to come and visit, so I went to California to stay with friends. They brought me to her house Dec. 23. Virginia and Joe were arriving then, too. All I saw was a short lady with long black hair...then she turned around and gave me a hug and a kiss and welcomed me! It was such a memorable moment, seeing Annette for the first time.

"As I often visited her, I became Uncle Nick to Gina, and there were times Annette called me that, too. She did sign my *Beach Party* poster 'To Uncle Nick.'"

Annette and Frankie were in Utica to perform their show in 1990, and on Nick's 45th birthday he got two special treats from Annette. "I was sitting next to her at Aunt Jo's table and all of a sudden Annette presented me with a Mickey Mouse watch and started singing Happy Birthday to me. Everyone chimed in. I was in seventh heaven."

During one of his visits to her home, he became suspicious that something was wrong with Annette. "I would watch her walk in the hallway, and she'd put her hand against the wall to steady herself," Nick recalls. "I thought she walked like an old lady. When I told her that I thought something wasn't right, she said she had dancer's knee and that she was trying herbal remedies to take care of it.

"Later, Virginia called me to tell me about Annette having MS. I knew all about MS because two of my neighbors had it, and I knew exactly what would happen to her. I just cried. I called my mom, then I called Aunt Mickie, who said, 'I wanted to tell you so many times but we promised we wouldn't say anything.'"

In 1992, shortly after Annette revealed in a USA Today interview that she had multiple sclerosis, Nick returned to California, this time as a photographer and videographer on a special assignment.

Nick Strange is a fan who became a close friend of Annette's after her family in Utica, N.Y., "adopted" him. (1992 photo: Bonnie Wendt)

"I was working with the MS Foundation in Utica (New York), so I filmed and took photos at Annette's house for the Utica newspaper. We screened it on her TV and she picked the video that she liked, which I submitted for the Utica TV promo. She also did a radio PSA for the Utica MS Walk," says Nick.

However, it wasn't all work and no play for Annette and Nick. Sharing their Italian heritage and love for Italian food, Nick played chef in Annette's kitchen.

"We had chicken riggies—an Italian-American pasta dish native to the Utica-Rome area of New York—and pasta fagioli, a traditional Italian soup made from pasta and beans. When I cooked for her, I'd say, 'If we don't like it, we'll throw it out and order pizza.' We laughed and talked about her relatives, like Uncle Windy, who was quite a character. Everything was so casual. We're Italians...it's just the way we are." Nick fondly remembers that "On one of my visits to Palm Springs, Virginia made meatballs like my mother made."

On Oct. 21, 1992, Nick was thrilled to attend the invitation-only awards ceremony honoring Annette, along with adult Mouseketeer Jimmie Dodd and Mooseketeer Roy Williams, as the newest Disney Legends. That night, several people ended up at Annette's house to celebrate her 50th birthday one day early—Nick videotaped the party for Annette. As a birthday gift, he had made a heart pin for her in solid sterling: a carved Mickey Mouse face that contained three hearts—one for each of her children. "She loved it and gave me a kiss," says Nick. "I also made a half-hour video of her life, intertwining recorded video of her aunts and uncle reminiscing, as well as using photos of Annette when she was very young, which we watched when things settled down."

Like most kids of the 1950s, Nick was a fan of the *Mickey Mouse Club*. And, like most fans, Annette became his favorite.

"She was an Italian girl and I'm an Italian guy. She stood out on the show because of her ethnicity, and that's what got me interested. But I did like all of the Mouseketeers, especially Sharon and Darlene," says Nick.

Annette left a deep impression on him.

"Annette laughed a lot," Nick remembers. "She was never negative, never talked about people and was always very complimentary. She was not a phony; what you saw was what you got. Annette was a truthful person and I never saw any ego in her."

Being the young fan of a TV show sent Nick on an extraordinary lifetime journey. He gained an extra family, met many other fans from across the country, and, to his amazement, became friends with the little Italian girl who captured his and millions of other viewers' hearts on the *Mickey Mouse Club*. The black-and-white TV screen turned into real life and gave him incredible memories, and he cherishes every single one.

Sharon Baird

Mouseketeer

Tiny, tap-dancing Mouseketeer Sharon Baird became fast pals with Annette when the *Mickey Mouse Club* began in 1955, and remained one of her best friends throughout her life. After the show ended, Sharon worked in Las Vegas and on several TV shows, including a stint as multiple costumed characters for Sid and Marty Krofft. She also took part in several Mouseketeer reunions and performed with some of her old friends during special appearances.

Sharon says that Annette was "as beautiful on the inside as she was on the outside," a girlfriend that she could do silly, fun things with. One of her memories involves both silliness and fun:

"One night after we were through shooting early, Dick Darley (our first director who we both had a crush on) saw Annette and me sitting on the floor singing a little ditty we had written to a patty-cake rhythm. He liked it so much he asked if we would film it. We got the giggles but muddled through it. It went like this:

> We are two Merry Mouseketeers,
> As merry as can be!
> And when we start to wiggle our ears,
> We sing and dance with glee!
>
> Now, Monday's "Fun With Music,"
> And Tuesday's "Guest Star Day,"
> And Wednesday brings a big surprise,
> But there's more on the way!
>
> 'Cause Thursday brings the circus
> From big top right to you!
> And Friday we go round them up,
> So bring your old lasso!!

From Maine to California,
Throughout the USA,
From coast to coast at
five o'clock,
The Mouseketeers will say,

We are two Merry Mouseketeers,
As merry as can be,
And when we start to wiggle our ears, we jump and laugh
with glee!

As they got older, Sharon and Annette broke out of the Mouseketeer image and engaged in typical teenage behaviors.

"We were Goody Two-Shoes on the *Mickey Mouse Club* set and never got into trouble," Sharon recalls. "But later on, in our teens, we would smoke at her house. We had cigarettes hidden in a little stuffed kitten that was on her bed. One night we were blowing smoke out the window and her mother yelled at us through the door, 'I know what you girls are doing in there!' That was probably the most mischievous thing we ever did!"

Sharon is semi-retired and lives in Reno, Nevada. She occasionally makes Disney-related appearances with some of the other Mouseketeers.

Mouseketeer Sharon Baird was a close, lifelong friend. She attended the Funicellos' 50th anniversary party in 1991. (Photo: Nick Strange)

Kevin Kidney

Disney Designer

Kevin Kidney, a designer of theme park shows and attractions for The Walt Disney Co. for 25 years, is the creative genius behind the special walking cane that was given to Annette in 1992. The cane's design was a collaboration of several people, and Kevin has the unique story behind making it and eventually meeting Annette.

When Annette went public with her MS in 1992, she was unsteady on her feet and walking with support. Disney wanted to do something nice for her, so studio publicist Arlene Ludwig and Director of Corporate Synergy Lorraine Santoli, who also were friends of Annette's, came up with the idea of creating a cane that reflected her career at Disney.

"The studio hadn't thought of a cane, but Annette's husband, Glen, said she really could use one," Kevin recalls. "Arlene didn't want to do anything to remind Annette of her illness, but Glen said she NEEDED a different cane. He said the one her doctor gave her was made of aluminum and was very institutional looking, which reminded her more of her illness. Annette said one reason she didn't like the cane was because it set off the alarms in airports. Glen said that if the cane came from the studio, it would mean so much more to her and remind her of friends and good times at Disney."

Lorraine filled out the proper form, which subsequently landed on Kevin's desk. "I remember the request form was dated Aug. 28, 1992, at the art department where I worked," says Kevin. "It went to my supervisor, and he said, 'This has to go to Kevin. There's no one who talks about and loves Annette as much as Kevin!' At the time I was a parade- and show-designer, so this was a special project. I was thrilled to take it! I had a week to work on it so I had a lot of questions, like how tall is she, what colors does she wear a lot, and of course one of them was purple. So I got out the color wheel and picked out complementary colors to purple—they're all on there."

Because Kevin was a fan, he knew Annette's favorite movie role was Mary in *Babes in Toyland,* and her first hit record was *Tall Paul.* He represented them with a record and a pull-toy horse, and added decorations that included the MMC logo, some Mouse Ears, ballet slippers and one of her most beloved Disney characters, Pluto.

"The only request I got from Lorraine and Arlene was to have their names and the names of the Mouseketeers around the bottom. They were very small, of course," Kevin laughs. "At the end of the week the cane was painted by a studio artist named Eric Heinz. He took a couple of days to paint the characters with enamel paints so they won't rub off or get scratched. Then he took the cane to the paint shop where they hung it on a wire and sprayed it with thick polyurethane, putting a hard shell on it. Eric and I also hid our initials on the cane...if you pull the rubber stopper off the bottom and look, there they are!"

About a week after the cane was finished, Disney had a dinner for Annette and presented it to her. Although Kevin wasn't at the dinner, he heard that Annette was deeply touched by the gift. "She was very teary and emotional and said, 'Gosh, it's like everything I love is on here! How did you know?' Annette asked Lorraine who the artist was so she could write a thank-you letter," says Kevin. A few days later a note in a little Mickey Mouse envelope appeared in Kevin's inbox. He was astounded. "I didn't know who it was from so I just tore it open and I thought, oh my God, is this for real?"

On Oct. 22 of that year, Annette would turn 50, and on her birthday she was to be presented with the Disney Legends Award at the studio. Kevin, assigned to art-direct the ceremony that year, built a set in Anaheim, then drove it to Burbank to assemble it. That's when he got a huge surprise.

"Lorraine's assistant came and got me and said 'Annette wants to meet you!'" says Kevin. "I thought, SHE wants to meet ME? I wanted to meet her! There she was, sitting on a park bench, when

Kevin Kidney designed Annette's Disney-character cane, which she loved. Kevin got to meet her in 1992. (Photo: Glen Holt)

we were introduced. She used the cane and stood up and gave me a hug. She said she was so happy to meet me and I thought, this is a dream! I wish I had my camera! Then Annette said she wanted a picture taken with me. Glen had brought his camera so he took a photo of me and Annette. Since it was on their camera I hoped that I would get it. Annette didn't forget me!"

The cane's painter, Eric, wasn't there that day, but a few months later he and Kevin got to see Annette at Disneyland, where she was doing a signing event. She posed for a photo with both of them, and Kevin came prepared for an autograph as well.

"I brought her first LP record, *Annette*, and she filled the whole pink space around her head on the cover! She kind of wrote me a letter, thanking me for my work, saying how meaningful it was. She was very, very sweet," the artist recalls. "Every time she'd appear on TV with the cane my mom would tape it and send it to me. People would ask her about the cane and she'd say her friends at Disney made it. It was absolutely wonderful. It was one of those projects you get that's out of the ordinary and ends up being very special. Annette was every bit herself, absolutely as sweet and sincere as she was in her films. She was a real person."

After 25 years at Disney, Kevin started his own design company, The Kevin & Jody Show, based in Anaheim. He and his colleague, Jody Daily, are designers, product creators, animators, illustrators and bloggers. They have contributed designs to many theme park shows and attractions, allowing Kevin a continued connection to Disney. A few years ago, Kevin created a stop-motion puppet image of Annette taken from the opening of the *Merlin Jones* movie. Several of his cartoon images of her are now distributed on products such as coffee mugs and T-shirts to benefit The Annette Funicello Research Fund for Neurological Diseases.

David Stollery

Actor and Engineer

David Stollery was a child actor who appeared in three popular *Mickey Mouse Club* serials: "The Adventures of Spin and Marty," "The Further Adventures of Spin and Marty," and "The New Adventures of Spin and Marty." He worked with his longtime friend Tim Considine in all of them, and with Annette in the latter two.

As a teenager, David left the acting profession. He turned in a new direction and entered the Art Center College of Design, where his studies led to a career in the automobile industry with General Motors and Toyota. The 1978 second generation A40 Series Toyota Celica is David's design. He now runs his own successful business making fiberglass lifeguard towers.

David says he didn't mind playing the "snotty rich kid" in the Disney serials, where he collected his own following of fans who loved him, if not his character, Marty Markham. He remembers Annette fondly.

"In the series, Tim and I really weren't working with the Mouseketeers on a daily basis, but we all went to school on the lot in the red trailer," he recalls. "Looking back, I remember how astonished I was at how professional the kids all were. They followed instructions and did the best they could with what they were asked to do. They were aware that they were paid to do a job and be respectful of Disney.

"It was apparent that Annette had a really big fan base—she stood out as a favorite with people. She was a genuinely nice person, there was nothing put on about her. She didn't try to work at presenting herself correctly, which was very different from all the rest of us. We tried to be extra nice because of the situation we were in, and I was amazed at how controlled and disciplined

Tim Considine (left), Annette and David Stollery in the
Mickey Mouse Club serial "The Further Adventures of Spin
and Marty," 1956. (Photo © The Walt Disney Company)

(the young actors) were at that age. With Annette there was no
pretense. She was this genuinely wholesome, nice young lady."

After Annette was diagnosed with MS, David was one of
many Disney friends who visited her at home.

"Two of the Mouseketeers, Doreen and Sharon, visited her
often, right up to when Annette passed away," David remembers. "When her MS progressed and she needed assistance, she
was very positive and gracious. There was no complaining—
she was the same Annette we had always known. And she still
looked gorgeous.

"During one visit she had a record album from when we were
working for Disney," says David, sharing a special memory.
"She said, 'Weren't we something?' Everybody understood the
person that she was, the way she handled a serious illness so
graciously the whole way through. Not many would handle it
that way. I can't think of anyone else in my life like that."

In 2006, David and Tim Considine were made Disney
Legends. They both spoke at Annette's Celebration of Life at
Disney Studios two months after her death in 2013, where David
offered the most memorable quote about his former co-star.

"Annette Funicello," he said, "was effortlessly genuine."

Lorraine Santoli

Disney Publicist and Director of Corporate Synergy

Imagine being a 7-year-old enthralled with the *Mickey Mouse Club* and fascinated by the show's singing, dancing Mouseketeers. Imagine getting a job at Disney and, 25 years later, meeting the famous Mice and working with them. Imagine, then, spending years as their traveling companion and publicity maven, becoming friends with them along the way. If that wasn't cool enough, imagine becoming best friends with Mouseketeer Sherry Alberoni and close friends with Annette Funicello. And, beyond that, writing a book about it all.

That's what happened to Lorraine Santoli, a little girl from Brooklyn who became a *MMC* fan like everyone else. But unlike most young unofficial Mouseketeers, she grew up and actually landed a job that was the envy of all of them. She looks back on her Disney days with awe, grateful for all of her opportunities at Disney but mostly for becoming the studio's Mouseke-Mascot.

"I think the first time I met Annette was on the set of the NBC-TV special *25 Years of Mouseketeers* in 1980 as the publicist for the show," says Lorraine. "I remember her being as nice and down-to-earth as she appeared to be on screen. It would be a few years before I got to know her well, although our paths would cross from time to time. Working at Disney Studios, I knew her brother, Mike Funicello, who also worked there for many years."

Traveling with Annette was among her duties, but it felt more like fun than work.

"I remember going down to Walt Disney World with her and her husband, Glen, where she appeared with several other original Mouseketeers as guests on *The New Mickey Mouse Club* that was shot on that property. Annette was always a pleasure to be with whether it was travel or just going out to dinner near her home in Encino," Lorraine recalls. "She always looked beautiful and ready to meet fans in the most generous way. I never, ever saw her turn down an autograph or not stop to speak with someone who approached her. She also had a great sense of humor and made me laugh a lot."

Lorraine remembers a special event in Washington, D.C., when Annette was honored by the national Order Sons of Italy, the largest and oldest Italian-American fraternal organization in the United States. "They treated her like a queen," says Lorraine. "She was just a bright light wherever she went. There wasn't a time when I was with her on our travels, or even at home when press came to interview her, that any men that were involved in the interview didn't say to her, 'I had the biggest crush on you!' She was always so kind and sweet to each and every one of them."

She was always well-received by fans, says Lorraine. "I attended a number of her concerts with Frankie Avalon when they were doing live shows all over the place and the fans went crazy when Annette took to the stage. While I don't think she loved being in the spotlight, she was always so happy to greet the fans that she met with smiles and kind words."

When Annette's autobiography, *A Dream Is a Wish Your Heart Makes: My Story*, came out in 1994, Annette, her parents and Lorraine took a trip to New York City—Lorraine's hometown. "I so wanted my mom, who lived in Brooklyn, to meet Annette. I was lucky enough to use the limo that was there for Annette and her family to pick up my mom at her home and bring her back to the Regency Hotel to meet the Funicellos. It was a thrill for my Italian mom who fit right in. Annette couldn't have been nicer to her," Lorraine recalls.

Lorraine also was able to spend some special moments with Annette out of the public eye. One occurred when Mouseketeer Sharon Baird was visiting Annette and Glen at home. "Annette, Sharon and I were in her kitchen at the house in Encino. Annette was washing dishes and Sharon was drying them. They were talking about the old days on the *Mickey Mouse Club* and suddenly they broke into their own version of "We Are the Merry

Mouseketeers" from the show. For me, having been a child of the *Mickey Mouse Club*, I was amazed that here I was, with Annette and Sharon, singing their own made-up lyrics to a *MMC* song just for me. It was wonderful!" (The lyrics are in Sharon's memories of Annette elsewhere in this book.)

Annette's close friends, Disney publicist Lorraine Santoli (top) and Mouseketeer Sharon Baird, at Gina's wedding rehearsal, 1994. (Photo: Nick Strange)

Some of Lorraine's favorite memories were the times that she and Annette spent together, just the two of them, before and after Annette's MS diagnosis.

"I used to have dinner with her every Tuesday evening because that's the day of the week that Glen would go up to his ranch in Bakersfield for a few days," Lorraine recalls. "We'd sit at the little round table in her living room and have pizza or Chinese food, sandwiches or pasta, and just talk about so many different things. Sometimes we'd go out for dinner to some of her favorite places near home. It was just two girlfriends having a girls' night out once a week, except that I got to do it with Annette, a person that I watched on TV as a kid and grew up with. Those were special days that I'll never forget.

"Of course, I also have many memories of her valiant fight with multiple sclerosis. Sadly, I saw her deteriorate over time. She always had hope that someday she would get better. I'll never forget something she once told me with regard to her illness and her love for the man that was like a second father to her, Walt Disney. When speaking of trying so many different courses of treatment that she hoped would help her condition, she said, 'I wish Mr. Disney were still here. He'd know what to do.'"

As a friend to all of the Mouseketeers, Lorraine offers her take on why Annette was so popular with *MMC* viewers.

"She just had IT, that special something that comes across the TV and movie screen that makes someone stand out from all the others. Annette was always asked that question and she always answered the same way, 'I don't know why I stood out. I wasn't the best singer, I wasn't the best dancer. Maybe it was because I was more ethnic looking than the others.'

"I don't think it had anything to do with ethnicity. She was charismatic and that came across. Some people just have it, and she did. She was as beautiful on the inside as she was on the outside and every move she made in life exemplified that. She never veered from that image because that's who she really was."

In 1995 Lorraine wrote *The Official Mickey Mouse Club Book*, a behind-the-scenes look at how the show began, reminiscences by the Mouseketeers and other exclusive info, with a foreword by Annette. She also wrote *Inside the Disney Marketing Machine* (Theme Park Press) in 2015. Lorraine retired from Disney in 2000.

Bonnie Kirn Wendt

Missouri Fan Club President

I started my Annette Funicello Fan Club in March of 1961 when I was 15 going on 16 after being fascinated by the little dark-haired girl on the *MMC* when I was younger. I didn't know much about fan clubs at the time—I'd never been in one and didn't know if Annette had one or not. I wrote her a letter and sent it to the Disney Studios, and much to my surprise, I received a reply from Annette, in her handwriting! She granted me my wish to start a club and sent three 8-by-10 photos and a bio to start, plus her *home address*!

To get members, I advertised in some of the movie magazines, and Rita Vandeveer joined. I found her to be fun and as much a fan as I was. She wanted to start a club, too, and I encouraged her. I finally met Rita in person when she came to St. Louis for a visit in the summer of 1964, and we wrote our first combined fan club journal on that visit.

Later that year we were both invited to Annette's wedding to Jack Gilardi on Jan. 9, 1965. Talk about being excited! We decided to do a combined fan club journal about the wedding and our trip to California. We both ran clubs for a while, but I was in college by then and becoming very busy. Soon after that, I sent my club members over to Rita's club to add to her members, and she did a terrific job of running the club for 28 years!

After many short visits with Annette during the years she was raising her children, we finally got to spend some real time together in March of 1989. Annette told me, "This is the year I am going to concentrate on friendship." Looking back on that, she knew of her MS diagnosis, but the rest of us did not. This was a very special trip for me, Lou Fitton and another fan.

Bonnie Kirn Wendt was a fan club president who spent a lot of
time with Annette over the years. (1990 photo: Nick Strange)

Our first day there, Annie took us shopping and bought each
of us whatever we wanted! It was a lovely shopping area with
tons of flowers and fountains all around. Riding in her Cadillac,
I have a great memory of her turning up the radio and singing
loudly to "Don't Worry, Be Happy!" Soon we were all singing!
At that time in her life, that is what she had decided to do. She
didn't let the illness take over while she could still enjoy life.

I decided on a shorts set in pale blue with white silk roses
for my gift from Annie. I still have it today and sometimes
wear it as pajamas. After our shopping excursion, we returned
to Annette's house where we had lots of laughs, took a zillion
pictures, and then Annette cooked us dinner! She fixed one of
her favorites, called chicken riggies. I loved it and asked for
the recipe. We then forgot about it, but a couple of weeks after
I returned home, here came the recipe, in her handwriting! I
still love making it and thinking of her.

We spent the next day at Disney Studios. That's really special
when you are with Annette Funicello! Arlene Ludwig, Disney
publicist and a friend of Annette's, took us to lunch while

Bonnie and Rita met Annette for the first time when they were invited
to her wedding to Jack Gilardi on Jan. 9, 1965. (Rita Rose Collection)

another lady gave us a tour. That evening Glen took us out to
dinner, along with Sharon Baird! (We sure did a lot of eating
on this trip!) Annette and Sharon were still very close and saw
a lot of each other, even though Sharon lived in Reno, Nevada.

The next afternoon was spent at Joe and Virginia's house.
I loved those people like my own parents—they were so welcoming and genuine. They had recently redecorated their home
and wanted to show us all around. Redecorating is something
Annette does often—mother and daughter LOVE to change
things up every now and then! Joe was home this day too, an
added delight!

Annette always made sure that any time we came to visit we
were well-entertained. Most trips included Virginia, who loved
doing things with us. She was so much fun, constantly relating
funny stories of things that had happened to the family. Many
of the stories were from her travels with Annette during her

"movie star" days. One of her favorite stories is about the fan who used to bake Annette cakes in the shape of open Bibles. "They were so fancy we didn't want to eat them!" Virginia said. Another was about a girl who took a bus to visit Annette and had to walk up the steep hill to their house. "She had to carry a washcloth with her because she thought she'd throw up with excitement!" Virginia told us.

That evening, we returned to Annette's to change to go out for dinner—just us girls! To make it extra special for us, Annie "borrowed" a limo to pick us up! It actually belonged to Fortes, the restaurant where we were going, which was one of Annie's favorites. We had drinks in the back and were tooling along, having a great time, when I noticed the phone had gotten knocked off and was hanging out the door! I watched it bang up and down along the highway and panicked! I told Annette, and she asked the driver to stop so we could pull it back inside. We then started giggling and couldn't stop! Annie loved to laugh, and always seemed to find the fun in every situation. I remember her saying, "I'd better give him a nice tip. He may have to replace the phone!" It turned out to be a lovely dinner with a lot of "girl talk."

The following day I had to leave for home. Lou was able to stay another day, so Annette had her move over to her house and she got to stay in Gina's room! On another trip, she had me do the same. It was great waking up and having coffee with Annie and Glen!

Through the years, one thing I've always noticed about Annette is that she is so interested in other people, especially normal, everyday people. She asked so many questions of us that it was hard for us to get her to talk about herself! It was that genuine interest in others that made her so special to her friends. I'm so glad I was chosen to be one of them.

Louis Pietroforte

Godson

Louis Pietroforte was an ordinary little boy whose picture kept showing up in movie magazines. That's what happens when your godmother is Annette Funicello.

Louis is the son of Joe and Dorothy "Dottie" Pietroforte, whose best friends were Joe and Virgie Funicello. He was born in 1962, when Annette was 20, and she immediately took to the little blond-haired baby. So did the fans, who loved seeing photos of Annette with Louis.

"Our families were very close. Our parents were always doing things together. They would go out almost weekly, and they went on vacations together. I really considered the Funicellos just like family," says Louis.

"As far as holidays went, we would go to their house every Christmas Eve. That was something that I always looked forward to because all of Annette's family would be there, and sometimes Jack's parents would be there. They were very family oriented, so it was always a very special occasion for me. I think that we did that up to the time Joe and Virgie sold their house in Encino and moved to Palm Springs."

Annette's love of babies, especially Louis, brought the families even closer as she began babysitting her very young godson.

"It's not something that I remember very well," says Louis. "She would either be at my house or I would go to Virgie and Joe's. A lot of what happened at that time came to me through stories, usually from Virgie as she liked to tease me. I guess one time I was at their house when I was very little and they had a fish tank. I must have watched Virgie feed the fish so I decided that I would feed them myself. Supposedly, I knocked over the whole fish tank! Virgie loved to tease me about that.

"When I was around a year old, *16 Magazine* did a photo spread of Annette babysitting me at my parents' house. I still have a copy of the magazine and the proof photos." Louis sometimes shows them to his high school English students, who, he says, get a big kick out of the fact that their teacher was in a teen magazine with a Disney star.

Having a celebrity as a babysitter didn't faze Louis. To him, she was just a family friend.

"To be honest, I can't remember when I realized that Annette was famous, but I can tell you that it did not have any effect on me," he recalls. "My parents were friends with Virgie and Joe before Annette became a Mouseketeer, and because they were always in our lives, I just never looked at her that way. I remember that her friends like Sharon (Baird) and Shelley (Fabares) would be around quite a bit and they would know me, but to me, that is all they were, Annette's friends.

"I remember times, as I got a bit older, sitting around a table at Joe and Virgie's house and talking to Annette, Sharon, my mom and Virgie about some things going on in my life. To me, they were just easy to talk to, not anyone famous. But one time, when I was about six years old, Jack and Annette took

Annette's mom, Virginia, and her godson, Louis Pietroforte, visited Annette on the set of *Muscle Beach Party* in 1964. (Photo: American International Pictures)

me to the premiere of *The Jungle Book*. There were news media there and they interviewed Annette on the way in. That's the only time I can remember being really aware that she was famous."

Louis credits Annette's whole family for being a great influence on him growing up.

"Because they were like family to me, I was always very comfortable being with them. They were always fun, and they were very caring and genuine people. I think that I learned a great deal by being around such good people during the formative part of my life," says Louis. "Annette was someone who was easy to talk to. As I got older and was in high school, I'd talk to her about issues that I was having, and she was very understanding."

Louis later moved to San Diego and married. Because of the distance, he didn't see Annette often. But, he says, "She was still involved in my life. My parents still were friends with Joe and Virgie and I would see Annette when the family got together, but it was not as often as in the old days. I have nothing but good memories of growing up and spending time with her."

Louis feels he was very fortunate to have Annette as his godmother and credits her with being a good role model for him. The last time he saw her was toward the end of her life, and he remains very thankful for that opportunity.

"I was up in L.A. visiting my dad. Annette's MS had really progressed; in fact, it was right before she passed away. It just so happened that Glen stopped by my dad's house to bring Annette to say hello, and it was just a coincidence that I was there and I got to see her. By that point, she was not able to speak, but I think she knew who my dad and I were. We talked to her for a bit and then they left. That was the last time I saw her.

"Maybe God wanted me to be there that day to be able to say goodbye to her."

Louis is an English teacher at Chula Vista High School in California. He is married and has one daughter.

Arlene Ludwig

Veteran Disney Publicist

Arlene Ludwig spent half a century helping to spin Disney magic as a publicist for The Walt Disney Company. She began her career in the New York Buena Vista office in 1962 as an assistant, and her first foray into publicity began with fan magazines. She then moved to California ten years later and eventually became West Coast Publicity Director.

Her first meeting with Annette came several years earlier when Arlene was in college. Her dad, Irving Ludwig, was already a Disney legend, having worked for the company since 1939 when he was hired to manage roadshow engagements of *Fantasia*. Later, he joined the distribution arm of Walt Disney Productions, and in 1959 he was named president of Buena Vista Distribution Co.

"I remember my dad wanting to introduce us, so when Annette was making an appearance on the East Coast while I was at Boston University, my father brought me over to meet her. I remember how cordial, warm and welcoming she was," says Arlene.

When *Merlin Jones* came out in 1964, Arlene was asked to join Annette on the road for her publicity tour. "That's when Annette and I became friends," Arlene recalls. "I made sure everything was going well. I was there to see she was well taken care of, that nothing was overlooked and we stuck to our schedule. I worked with the field agencies to assure that everything ran smoothly."

Arlene remembers Annette as being reliable and respectful on the road. "She was there to do a job and she did it. I enjoyed traveling with her as friends but I also had a job to do. We were two friends traveling together with business in between. Still, it was nice to care for the person you're traveling with. Annette's mom, Virginia, traveled with her on other publicity appearances."

One of Arlene's favorite memories was during a publicity stop in Denver. Annette wanted to get her hair done in the hotel salon where they were staying.

"Annette was just crazy about the Beatles," Arlene says. "Frank Petraglia, who handled all of the field publicity on the tours, was an Italian from New York, so Annette sort of adopted him as an uncle. We're sitting in the salon and Frank walks in wearing a Beatles wig! I have never seen her crack up the way she did—she literally could not stop laughing. It totally broke her up. I can still see Frank in that Beatles wig and it makes me laugh all over again. We didn't have cell phones then but it would have been great to have a photo of that moment!"

Annette and her agent, Jack Gilardi, were married Jan. 9, 1965, and Arlene was one of her seven bridesmaids. Later that year Annette was supposed to tour for *The Monkey's Uncle* and Arlene was scheduled to go on the road with her. "Then she told me she was pregnant, and the tour was cancelled." Arlene says.

Disney publicist Arlene Ludwig had a working relationship and longtime friendship with Annette. She was one of seven bridesmaids in Annette's 1965 wedding to Jack Gilardi. (1989 photo: Rita Rose Collection)

One anecdote Arlene recalls was when Annette went to see a publisher about writing her autobiography. "She talked to the publisher and regaled him with wonderful stories about her life. He said, 'Now, what's the *real* scoop?' and she said there's no scoop. They were looking for dirt and scandals. But there weren't any, she had a very normal life with supportive parents. He said thanks but no thanks. Later she went on to do a book the way she wanted to tell her story."

Annette's autobiography, *A Dream is a Wish Your Heart Makes: My Story*, co-authored by Patricia Romanowski, came out in 1994 and was later made into a TV movie.

When Annette was diagnosed with multiple sclerosis in 1987, she kept it a secret for five years. In 1992, Arlene and Disney's Director of Corporate Synergy, Lorraine Santoli, collaborated on who they felt should break the story and decided to go to Tom Green of *USA Today*.

"Tom was a respected journalist and we felt that *USA Today* was the place to go. We told him we wanted him to talk to Annette, that she had a story and we wanted it to come from her," Arlene recalls. "She trusted him to help her come out about the MS, and he treated her story with dignity and respect. Once the story broke, the floodgates opened, and we organized her appearances on *Entertainment Tonight* and other TV shows."

In later years, when her MS had made her bedridden and unable to speak, Annette's second husband, Glen Holt, brought her to the studio to buy a Mickey Mouse watch and Arlene was asked to help him. "He asked if I'd like to see Annette and took me to the van. When he opened the back of the van and I said hello, she answered by blinking her eyes. It was so heartbreaking," says Arlene.

From Disney to the AIP beach movies to motherhood, Annette's appeal remained steady, Arlene notes. "Annette was what she was, and people adored her for that. No one called her goody-two-shoes. She had her own agenda. It was a private agenda and it didn't have anything to do with anyone else."

Arlene was honored at the 49th annual Publicists Awards Luncheon on Feb. 24, 2012, to commemorate her 50th anniversary with the Walt Disney Company.

David Kessel

Musician and Record Producer

In 1961, Annette made her first—and only—Christmas record, paired with longtime friend and beach movie actor/singer Frankie Avalon. "Together We Can Make a Merry Christmas" was a 45 single, backed by Frankie's recitation of "The Night Before Christmas." Lyrics and music were written by Keith Droste, Frankie's musical conductor, who brought it to his publisher, B.J. Baker, with the suggestion that it would be a good fit for Annette and Frankie.

B.J. was Betty Jane Baker, a top vocalist in Hollywood who sang backup on many of Annette's records, as well as those of other artists of the era. Formerly married to actor Mickey Rooney, she later wed jazz guitarist and music producer Barney Kessel and became stepmother to his sons, David and Dan. The sons, also in the music business, were asked to co-produce the Christmas song on Pacific Star, their family record label.

In the late 1970s, David and Dan became immersed in the Southern California punk music scene and produced numerous recordings with many classic, punk and new wave bands and artists. In what seems like an odd twist in Annette's musical career, the Kessels thought she might fit into that scene, or at least complement it.

David has fond memories of working with Annette on the record project.

"When my brother, Dan, and I got involved in the whole L.A. punk movement, it became trendy to be retro. So when Frankie and Annette's Christmas record came along, we thought, 'We have this great song, and who doesn't like Frankie and

Annette?' I thought it was really cool because I felt the new culture would embrace them," says David.

"My brother and I were over at her house a lot, talking and going over mixes. It was really, really something else to hang out with Frankie and Annette, really trippy! It was kind of surreal, hanging out with Frankie and Annette at her house to make a record. They were such nice, professional people. Once she had on a really cool purple dress and I thought, 'She isn't a Mouseketeer anymore.'"

David says that working with Annette was easy because she had no ego.

"She was sweet and had a highly professional attitude toward what we were doing," he recalls. "She was well-trained. I give Walt Disney and her parents all the credit. Music is a tough business, and dirty, but she held herself with dignity and no ego. She was totally a pleasure to work with, and it was an unexpected treat for us to work with Frankie and Annette together. They both adapted very well to blending the old with the new."

And thus, the Kessels brought Annette and Frankie into a new music world. They hooked up with their friend, Rodney Bingenheimer, the iconic DJ of L.A. radio show "Rodney on the ROQ at WKRQ." A big fan of Annette's, he often played her hits and beach tunes and later had a small role in *Back to the Beach*.

"I took Annette and Frankie to Rodney's show and brought in Debbie Harry of Blondie on the phone from New York to talk on the air," says David. "We also called up Casey Kasem to promote the record on his Top 40. It was really fun to cross-promote the traditional Annette and Frankie crowd with the punk and new wave crowd, just to give them their place in history. They deserve their cultural relevance in history."

Like others who worked with Annette during her recording years, David's assessment of Annette's singing fell in line with those who observed her developing talent despite her insecurities.

"You can get very shy about vocals; it's innate to have insecurities. Annette conquered that," David says. "What really impressed me was her stability. At Sunset Sound studios, which was started by her longtime producer, Tutti Camarata, Annette was backed by the finest Hollywood musicians and background singers. It was a highly professional team of adults backing her up. The triple tracking—where you record the song three times—helps magnify the voice and give it a presence. It blends the sound in more and enhances it for those who aren't singers. And Annette was always enunciative. She said Mr. Disney told her she should always be clear and articulate."

After the release of "Together We Can Make a Merry Christmas," the Kessels tried to get Annette a recording contract with RCA Nashville to do country music, but the interest wasn't there, says David. However, in 1984, *The Annette Funicello Country Album*, which used Nashville musicians, was released on Starview Records, a sub-label of Fektive Records.

David Kessel has a wide musical niche in Hollywood. He runs several different music and media companies, hosts a radio show called Dave the K's Rockin' Surfer Show, owns music-related website CaveHollywood and has his own band, Willapa. He describes himself as a "musical renaissance man."

Dan Kessel

Musician and Record Producer

As a musician and vocalist I've worked on recordings with John Lennon, Bob Dylan, Phil Spector, Celine Dion and Cher, and I produced records featuring The Ventures, The Ramones, Blondie, etc. While they were all wonderful, my fondest memories are of working with Annette. But years before that happened, our paths had already crossed on several occasions.

My former stepmother (and later my dear friend), Betty, who worked professionally as B.J. Baker, was a top Hollywood vocal contractor and vocalist who sang backup on the records of Elvis, Frank Sinatra and Johnny Cash, among others. She sang on all of Annette's hit records ("Tall Paul," "Pineapple Princess," etc.) as well as those of Annette's contemporaries such as Shelley Fabares, Frankie Avalon and Paul Anka. Betty was the second wife of actor Mickey Rooney and was the mother of Mickey's first two children, Mickey Jr. and Timothy Rooney. It was through her that I met Annette years later.

One summer evening in 1963 I bought a ticket for a double feature at one of the theaters on Hollywood Boulevard. I can't remember what movies were showing but it included a "sneak preview" afterwards, at no additional cost. I asked at the ticket booth what the preview was and they wouldn't tell me, saying "It's a SNEAK preview. We can't inform the public what it is." It seemed mysterious so I was determined to stay late and check it out.

There was a small section of choice seats reserved and roped off in the middle of the theater. Suddenly, my teenage mind got blown when Annette Funicello, flanked by guys in suits, was escorted into the reserved VIP section. I couldn't believe it was really her, right there, so close. I was quietly freaking out. Immediately, the lights went dim and the curtains parted, revealing the opening strains of "Beach Party." When it was over, Annette stood up and acknowledged the audience with a big smile. Then she blew a kiss to the audience and was whisked out of there, presumably into a waiting limo. The whole unexpected experience was pretty amazing to me. Annette was a star that night. She was a star every night.

Going back a few years: A successful audition arranged by their then-stepfather, Buddy Baker (head of the music department at Disney Studios), resulted in my talented stepbrothers, Tim Rooney and Mickey Rooney, Jr., being signed as original Mouseketeers. However, their tenure was short-lived. They and their fellow Mouseketeer, actor Paul Petersen, were all let go early after the three of them were caught getting into mischief on the set, playing with paint and brushes left by the crew. It was a sad moment for all, but they were invited back years later with the others for the 1980 Mouseketeer reunion special.

The first time I met Annette, along with the Beach Boys, was in 1965 on the set of *The Monkey's Uncle*. I accompanied my stepbrother, Tim, who was a guest on the set. Tim had been a working actor in movies and TV since age 10. He already knew Annette from the early Mouseketeer days and knew the Beach Boys' lead guitarist, Carl Wilson, from Hollywood Professional School where Mickey Jr. went. Also, Buddy Baker was writing the film score for the movie.

This was a huge deal for me back then. As a young teen, I was thrilled to meet Annette, who always held an almost magical charm for me. Like millions of other guys my age, I'd had a crush on her for years. So meeting her was a dream come true, especially since she was warm and welcoming and spent as much time with us as she could. She was lovely, talented, hard-working and cheerful as she soldiered through some relentless and exhausting hours of work. Others may have complained of unending takes, dancing and singing under bright, intensely hot lights, but not Annette. She took it all in stride. And, she was noticeably a better dancer than her on-screen dance partner, Beach Boys lead singer Mike Love.

Music producers Dan Kessel (left) and David Kessel worked
with Annette and Frankie on their Christmas single. (Photo:
Theresa Kereakes, © Dan Kessel Productions).

It wasn't until 1981 that I finally got to work with her on the
record "Together We Can Make a Merry Christmas," a duet with
Frankie Avalon. When it came time to call our first meeting to
define our production vision and refine our plans, Annette sug-
gested it take place in her home. I arrived with my brother David
and our production coordinator, Blake Xolton, at her front door,
in suit and tie with briefcase in hand, on time at 8 a.m.

When Annette answered the doorbell and invited us in, I
was immediately awestruck at how stunningly lovely she was.
When I'd met her before in the studio, she looked great, but
this was on a whole other level. This was beyond a beach party
gal. This was more like Loretta Young or Hedy Lamarr. She
was immaculately groomed and looked absolutely perfect.
Her hair looked perfect. Her clothes looked perfect. Her
home looked perfect. Complementary shades of lavender and
purple were tastefully interspersed throughout her clothing
and the home decor. She was very gracious, inviting us to sit
down in her beautiful living room and offering us coffee and

pastry on a large silver tray. That was just what the doctor ordered, right about then.

She joined us for coffee, sitting down on the sofa next to me. After we had visited a bit, I commented on something on a large table in an adjacent room. It bore a kind of resemblance to the Mickey Mouse hats still available at Disneyland, but in a strange color.

I opened my briefcase and pulled out a legal pad full of pre-production ideas to discuss. As we talked them over, invariably one, then another of her three children would appear fleetingly nearby in the kitchen and Annette would excuse herself, bring them out and introduce them to us, then go back into the kitchen with them. They were all getting ready to go to school and she made sure they had breakfast, and that they had their lunches to take with them. Very nice kids they were, and what a great mom she was. In between kitchen moments with them, she would apologize for the interruption and attempt to re-engage with us and pick up where she had left off. Because of all the breaks in continuity she would basically have to start over again each time.

When the kids had all left the house for school, she relaxed and said, "I know we have all of these details to go over but wouldn't you really rather just have a nice breakfast?" Of course, we opted for breakfast with her and had such a great time. She was a class act who was also a lot of fun to be with. When it was time to leave, I simply left her with a brief outline of everything I'd planned to go over with her. I told her to just give it a glance and let me know if she had any questions or comments. As it turned out, she was perfectly fine with everything.

We were together on numerous occasions after that, including the production of the record, the picture sleeve photo shoot, at KTLA TV in Hollywood with the honorary "mayor of Hollywood," Johnny Grant, setting up her appearance with Frankie Avalon at the Santa Claus Lane Parade on Hollywood Boulevard, and a host of other related activities. Aside from that, we also attended dinner parties in each other's homes.

While working in the recording studio together, I asked Annette and Frankie if they would mind recording a short, 10-second station I.D., plugging our friend Rodney Bingenheimer's weekend radio show, "Rodney on the ROQ," on station KROQ in L.A. We got it done in one or two takes. Rodney beamed when we delivered the tape to him. He loved it and played it on his show all the time. This ultimately led to his appearing, years later, in their movie *Back to the Beach*. He still has a radio show on Sirius XM.

My brother and I were credited on "Together We Can Make a Merry Christmas" as Dan Phillips and David Scott. We used those names for a few years, and in 1984 we reverted to our real names. I am the sole owner of those recordings with Annette and Frankie and I also own the song publishing.

Rodney Bingenheimer
Radio DJ

During a record show in a huge tent over a parking lot in Hollywood, Rodney Bingenheimer exclaimed in a deep and very West Coast surfer voice: "Annette is GOD, man!"

That was no surprise to listeners of KROQ in Los Angeles in the 1970s and '80s when Rodney was one of the most instinctive and iconic disc jockeys of the era. He was known as "Rodney on the ROQ" and "the mayor of the Sunset Strip" as he played punk, new wave and other cutting edge music. He helped many bands such as Blondie, the Ramones, the Sex Pistols and Duran Duran become successful in the American market.

And, he played Annette.

Incongruous? Not really.

Rodney got hooked on surf music in the '60s when he was a Hollywood groupie who loved Annette's beach movies.

"I watched all of her movies and have always been a fan," he recalls. "I went to the premiere of *Muscle Beach Party* and got her autograph, along with Jody McCrea's. It was the first time I met her and I liked her right away.

"I started playing her songs on the radio in the '80s and people loved it. Her music sounded very new wave. I got one of the evening DJs, April Whitney, to play her music, too. I always played 'Beach Party' around Easter—it starts out 'Easter vacation just started today.' I also played other pop classics from the '60s because I always thought they were fun as a kid."

Annette and Rodney struck up a friendship in 1981 when record producers Dan and David Kessel brought her duet with Frankie Avalon, "Together We Can Make a Merry Christmas,"

to his studio. He interviewed them on the air, adding a call-in
from Debbie Harry of Blondie, a nod to the record's new wave
crossover effect.

When Rhino Records put out *The Best of Annette* album in
1984, the producers tapped Rodney for his input.

"They contacted me because they knew I was such a big fan
and was playing her on the radio," he says. "I picked out the
cuts and included several beach movie tracks. Then I made a
clock out of the picture disc version."

A few years later, Annette brought Rodney on board for a
cameo role in *Back to the Beach*.

"Annette got me in that movie," he says. "I had Annette and
Frankie on my show and (surf rock guitarist) Dick Dale called
in to be interviewed. She even helped me get my SAG card so

Disc jockey Rodney Bingenheimer had Annette and Frankie
Avalon on his show after their release of "Together We Can Make
a Merry Christmas" in 1981. Rodney still loves to play Annette's
surf music on Sirius XM. (Photo © Dan Kessel Productions)

now I get to vote on the movies every year! I hung out with her on the set, which was really cool."

Annette's rendition of the song "Jamaica Ska" had a big impact on the California music scene, Rodney notes. It was one of the tracks on her *Bikini Beach* album in 1964, and she gave it new life when she sang it in *Back to the Beach* with Fishbone.

"In the late '80s there was a big ska thing happening in Orange Country with bands like No Doubt and Goldfinger," says Rodney. "The Ska Kings' version was one of the original ska songs done so well in '60s. Annette's version fit right in."

It was during the filming of *Back to the Beach* that Annette, having trouble walking in the sand, received her MS diagnosis. After she went public with that disability, Rodney again connected with her, and in 1992 became part of creating a special honor for her.

"My friend Keith Belinsky, who would do movie reviews on my show, helped me get Annette nominated for a star on the Hollywood Walk of Fame," says Rodney. "We called the Chamber of Commerce and had people write in. I don't know who paid for it. I was with her when she got her star in 1993, and years later I got a star."

In 2017, after 41 years at KROQ, Rodney was let go by the station. Soon after, he joined SiriusXM's *Little Steven's Underground Garage.*

Does he still play Annette's music? Oh, yeah. It's in his DNA.

"On October 22, her birthday, I still play 'Swingin' and Surfin' and 'Pineapple Princess.' The listeners love it and I still get letters and requests."

Sherry Alberoni Van Meter

Mouseketeer

One of the youngest Mouseketeers, Sherry Alberoni joined the *Mickey Mouse Club* as a second-season replacement on the Blue Team. Post-*MMC*, she appeared on many TV shows, including *The Farmer's Daughter, Ripcord, My Three Sons, The Man from U.N.C.L.E.* and *The Monkees,* with her biggest recurring role on *Family Affair.* As an adult, she had a long show business career both acting and providing voices for cartoon characters. In 1971 she married Dr. Richard Van Meter. They have two daughters and several grandchildren.

Sherry and her brother, Roy, were big fans of the *Mickey Mouse Club* before auditioning for the show together.

"On October 3rd, 1955, when the *Mickey Mouse Club* first appeared on ABC, my brother Roy and I, like every other child in America, had on our little plastic Mickey Mouse ears and were glued to the television set," she recalls. "I immediately loved all the Mouseketeers but my favorite wasn't Annette—she didn't stand out to me because she looked like all my Italian cousins in Cleveland. Of course, I thought she was pretty and a wonderful ballerina, but my favorites were Darlene and Cubby."

Sherry was familiar with the acting profession. "Roy and I had done quite a bit of television work—mostly commercials and small parts in serials. We had an agent who called one day and told my mom to take Roy to Walt Disney Studios to audition for the *MMC*. She thought I was too young."

But the Mouseketeer-to-be snagged an audition anyway, thanks to her brother and because of a unique talent she had perfected.

"Roy was a drummer and tap dancer, and after auditioning, he was told they already had Cubby, who was a drummer and tap dancer. They asked if he could play another instrument and Roy said, 'No, but I have a little sister who can play the trumpet and do a tap dance at the same time.' The casting director asked to see me, so the next day my mom took me to the Burbank studios. I played 'All of Me' on the trumpet as I tap danced—I almost knocked out all my teeth, but I got the job!"

Eventually, Annette and Sherry, the two Italian Mice, became fast friends.

"With names like Funicello and Alberoni, Annette and I bonded, and she called me her 'little sister.' That's when I fell in love with her, when I got to know her and saw how kind and friendly and sweet she was. She certainly didn't think she was a star and she acted just like all the other kids," says Sherry.

Their mothers became friends, too, as they car-pooled with their daughters to the studio.

"My family and I lived in Westchester (by the Los Angeles Airport) and my mom didn't drive, so my dad would take us to Annette's house in Encino and Virginia would drive Annette,

Mouseketeers Sherry Alberoni and Bobby Burgess saw Annette at Knott's Berry Farm in 1990. (Photo: Nick Strange)

my mom and me to the Walt Disney Studios where we went to
school for three hours each day," says Sherry. "We had one hour
for lunch and recreation and four hours of filming, rehearsing,
make-up, hair, wardrobe and everything else that goes into
filming a TV show.

"I really looked up to the 'big kids' because Karen, Cubby,
Moochie and I were considered the 'little kids.' I really
enjoyed dancing and singing with the Mice. I still have—and
cherish—an original Mouseketeer girl doll Annette gave me
for my birthday."

Sherry has fond memories of performing with Annette on
the 25th anniversary Mouseketeer Reunion show in 1980. And
she got to dance with the Red Team!

"When we did *The Mouseketeer Reunion* show on CBS I had
a lot of fun with Annette. Suddenly, I was the second tallest
(Annette was the tallest) of the girls who did the bulk of the
singing and dancing in that show, so in the lineup we were
placed next to each other. During rehearsals and filming I
got to see her fun sense of humor—we laughed a lot and we
were all constantly teasing each other. For several years we
did reunion shows at Disneyland and Disney World, and sometimes Annette would join us on stage. Of course, the audience
loved it," Sherry recalls.

"When we did the *New Mickey Mouse Club*, which filmed in
Florida, Annette did the show with us. One day she called us
all together and told us that she was diagnosed with multiple
sclerosis. She wanted us to hear it from her rather than read
that she 'had a drinking problem,' which is the story a tabloid
newspaper was going to print. Everyone was upset and sad and
very protective of her as we finished filming the show."

Throughout her life, Sherry has donated her time to a
variety of worthy causes. She took part in the Mouseketeer
live performances at Disneyland in the 1980s and has became
a fixture on Mouseketeer personal appearance tours that
began in the late '80s and continue today. In 2014, she received
a Disney Legend Award from the Disneyana Fan Club.

Patrick Cardamone
Cousin

When a famous cousin comes for a visit, sometimes you have to throw people off your lawn.

Especially when that cousin is Annette Funicello.

Patrick Cardamone, who owns a software consulting firm in New York state, is Annette's first cousin on her father's side. Patrick's mother was Elsie Funicello Cardamone, the only girl in a family that included brothers Joe, Sarge and Bob. Joe and Virginia had moved to California and were raising their family there while Patrick, several years younger than Annette, grew up in Mattydale, a suburb of Syracuse.

Annette had been the flower girl at his parents' wedding, and Patrick didn't meet her until years later, when she flew to Syracuse for a personal appearance, accompanied by her mother.

"I would have been around 10," Patrick recalls. "They came to our house in Mattydale, and when word got out that Annette was at our house, there were 500 people in our yard! They were trying to stuff notes in the window to get her autograph. My father had to go out and disperse the crowd. We were like being held prisoners in the house."

A few months later, Annette sent them tickets to the *Babes in Toyland* opening in Syracuse. "She always sent stuff to my mom, like a new record album. But she was just one of the family, hanging out, when she came to visit. She was such a family person," says Patrick. "She talked about Walt Disney and Dick Clark, and she loved babies. She would always pick up a baby if there was one around."

When he was 13, Patrick and his family moved to Utica, where Annette was born and many of her extended family members still resided.

Annette was the flower girl for Joe Funicello's
sister, Elsie, when she married Joe Cardamone in
1949. (Photo: Patrick Cardamone Collection)

"A lot of kids thought it was really cool that she was my cousin," says Patrick. "They knew she was from Utica and that my mom was a Funicello. I didn't do any fan stuff, just collected her records."

Over the years, Annette and her parents visited Utica several times. In 1981, when Patrick's sister Rose got married, Annette, her mom Virginia and daughter Gina attended the wedding in Utica. "Annette tried to stay in the background and let my sister be the star...that's just how she was. I remember she wore a nice beige, lacy dress," says Patrick.

Another recollection of that event was that sometimes fans can get a little crazy. "One lady came up to Annette in church with a tissue and tried to get her lipstick print! Then, we were sitting at a bar and somebody came to get an autograph from her. He was shaking so badly he dumped his drink in her lap!"

In 1995, Patrick had the opportunity to speak at a conference in California. He brought his mom along, and they spent one night with Joe and Virgie in their new Palm Springs home.

"Annette was there and she really fell in love with my daughter, Jilli, who was 5. I spent more time with Uncle Joe in his garage looking at his Cadillac. They brought in dinner from their favorite Italian restaurant, and we spent a lot of time laughing and talking about our grandparents and other relatives in Utica."

Patrick recalls the last time he saw his cousin, and how he, his wife and his daughter turned down a dinner invitation with a famous singer so they could spend time with family.

"We went to Palm Springs in 1997 and stayed with Virgie and Joe for a few days. They let us sleep in Annette's round bed," he says. "Virgie and Joe lived on a celebrity golf course. They would cut up cheese and sit on the patio with drinks, and the celebrities would come over. We were all sitting outside watching the golfers and Mike Connors came by and saw Annette. He immediately stopped golfing and sat down with her, then gave me his golf cart and said to go and play for as long as I wanted. He had a luxury cart with a full bar and air conditioning! And it went fast. When I got back, they were all still eating.

"Later, they asked if we would like to go to dinner with Frank Sinatra! But I didn't really care, I just wanted to hang out with Virgie and Joe. Uncle Joe took us to Indio to get some delicious California dates. He had a new Cadillac; it was the only car he drove."

Even though Annette grew up in California, she was interested in what was going on with her Utica relatives, says Patrick.

"Annette always liked to talk to us about our families and what we were all up to. She wanted to know all about my brothers and sisters and what their kids were doing. She asked about my sister Rose and said how much she enjoyed her wedding in Utica. I saw Annette maybe 10 times in my life," Patrick recalls, "and each one was so memorable."

Those fond memories include the delight of having a down-to-earth celebrity as his cousin—and how her fans had to be chased off the family's lawn.

Jackie Musgrave

Alaska Fan

I fell in love with Annette the first time I saw her on the *Mickey Mouse Club*. The show had been on for a while before we got it in Anchorage, but I was primed—a friend in California had sent me two issues of the *MMC Magazine* and Annette just looked like someone I wanted to know. When I saw the program, and watched her singing and dancing, the deal was sealed—Annette, whether she knew it or not, became one of my best friends. I loved everything she did on the show, and I spent my allowance on movie magazines that featured her.

She was my favorite teen actress, so I was thrilled when *The Shaggy Dog* was released and I could see her on the big screen. I wanted her to live next door; I envied those who could see her in person at Disneyland appearances. Alaska was too far from California, and she never came this far north, much to my disappointment.

I did meet her many years later, in 1972, when I was privileged to join my friend Rita Rose on a visit to Annette's home. She was gracious and welcoming, but what impressed me most was not the tour she gave us of her beautiful house, or the friendly conversation we had over the course of a couple of hours, or the way she was just like any other mom with her kids.

There were two things that stood out during that visit: She had bought a special cake for us to share at her kitchen table, and when my parents came to pick us up, she walked out to the truck with us to meet them. For me, those two gestures were the core of Annette's personality. She actually was the everyday neighbor next door who had a genuine interest in

Fan Jackie Musgrave came all the way from Alaska to
visit Annette with Rita in 1972. (Photo: Rita Rose)

others, and she possessed a caring, thoughtful heart even for
those she didn't know.

I never got into the beach movies. For me, Annette will
always be the cheerful Mouseketeer, offering her wide smile
and sparkling eyes in a joyful welcome to all. I was saddened
by her diagnosis of MS and her subsequent death, but she
lives on in DVDs, recordings, scrapbooks and those old *MMC*
Magazines...and most especially in my memory of how she
took time to not only open her home to two fans, but to stand
in her driveway and visit with my parents.

That was true grace.

Greg Ehrbar
Disney Writer

If you want to know anything about Walt Disney music and records, Greg Ehrbar is your go-to guy. A Los Angeles-based freelance writer and TV/video producer with two Grammy nominations, Greg is a former Disney staff writer who also did marketing for Disneyland, Walt Disney World and Shanghai Disneyland. Additionally, Greg served as writer/editor for DisneyMusicEmporium.com and *Twenty-Three*, Disney's in-studio magazine. Today he divides his time between Disney, Warner Bros. and Universal studios and independent projects.

He also was a fan of the *Mickey Mouse Club* and Annette.

"I love Disneyland, where the Mouseketeers and Walt Disney were," he says. "There's still a vibe to that...it's hard to describe the intimacy of it, the smaller, communal aspect that no other theme park has. You can actually go and look at the Sleeping Beauty Castle that you saw on TV."

Greg possesses great insight into the music of Disney, including Annette's many recordings on the Disneyland and Buena Vista labels. Co-author of *Mouse Tracks: The Story of Walt Disney Records* (University Press of Mississippi, 2006), he credits the prolific songwriting team of Richard and Robert Sherman and the musical vision of producer Tutti Camarata for making Annette's recording career a success...that, and Annette's unassuming attitude toward her musical abilities.

In the book, Tutti Camarata recalls that, "Annette was wonderful. But she was very nervous when we started making her records. You can really hear her voice develop from album to album as she gained confidence."

Greg agrees. "Annette progressed as a performer even though, when she started out, she still insisted 'I don't sing!' What endeared her to us, what made her so refreshingly unlike other singers, was her self-effacing nature," he says. "She was shy at first, not a great singer or actress but a good dancer. But she was guided, and to this day, other performers are guided—this is not new by any stretch.

"In her recordings, between her first album, *Annette*, and her last for Disney, *Something Borrowed, Something Blue*, you can hear how much vibrato she developed. Musically, she could have pursued more singing, but that wasn't what she was looking to do in her life. A lot of things were changing, popular music was changing, and it was the end of that particular brand of teen pop."

Greg notes that Annette's records had a huge impact on the Disney Company's fortune.

"The reason the company's Disneyland and Buena Vista labels stayed was because of Annette and the influence she had on entertainment," he says. "Without Annette, they wouldn't have had the Sherman Brothers, which led to the music for *The Parent Trap* and *Mary Poppins*. I've called Annette the Queen of Walt Disney World because, directly or indirectly, she had a hand in the existence of the park because of her singing career. Without the Shermans, *Mary Poppins* wouldn't have been the success it was — and box-office profits from *Mary Poppins* helped buy the land and build the Walt Disney World Resort. In her way, Annette had a major influence on where the company went and what we enjoy today."

Greg emphasizes that the public—Annette's fans—played a big role in making her music popular.

"I've done a presentation on Annette and teen stars, and one of the things that I emphasized was that the public chose Annette because of the song 'How Will I Know My Love,' which she sang in the MMC's 'Annette' serial. The record sold 600,000 copies and Walt said, 'You're gonna be a recording star.' Annette really wasn't sure about the whole thing, but Walt had the perfect musical staff in place, not only to present Annette in the best way possible, but also to keep her comfortable during the process.

"The public doesn't get enough credit sometimes for choosing pop stars. The public WANTED her. She was not a major star; she stood in the back until the public noticed her. If she didn't have that special quality, the 'Annette' serial would have come and gone. It wasn't a matter of can she sing. Simon Cowell said there are many great singers in studios but you have to have the whole package, and Annette had qualities that made her a performer—personality and voice—that even a better singer wouldn't have had."

Greg became a member of Annette's fan club in the 1970s, and he finally got to meet her in 1989 after he began working for Disney.

"I met Annette briefly at the Disney/MGM Studios opening in 1989. I was working the press event and my future wife, Suzanne, and I were at the park during the ceremony. Bob Hope and (Disney's then-CEO) Michael Eisner were there. It was unforgettable and exciting.

"Annette was only a few feet behind us, and we were instructed to not to talk to any celebrities, but there she was! Suzanne said, 'If you don't do this you'll regret it the rest of your life!' I thought, OK, the ceremony was over and everyone was mingling. It was right after her Armanino pasta sauce came out. Glen was there, so I thought maybe I'd talk to him first. That worked, and then he introduced me to Annette. I was struck by how frail and small she was. We chit-chatted and I asked about her sauce. I said *Italiannette* was my favorite LP and she said, 'Really?' I was glowing from that point on. And Suzanne assured me that I didn't sound stupid!"

Janet Almanzi Lundy

New York Fan

From a 1962 Annette Fan Club journal:

When I was a teenager, I always had dreams of meeting Annette, but I never thought it would really happen. But then, one day it did!

It all started with radio station WNDR in Syracuse, New York. They were running a contest with the unbelievable prize of meeting Annette. She was going to be in Buffalo—about 200 miles from me—for a personal appearance in conjunction with *Babes in Toyland*. I had to send my name, address, age and a snapshot of myself to enter the contest, and I was shocked when the radio station called to tell me I had won! Then they announced it on the radio, so I knew this was really going to happen!

A few weeks later, there we were, actually standing next to Annette Funicello at the Sheraton Hotel in Buffalo. I was with another contest winner from Syracuse and several teenage reporters from Buffalo schools, but I only had eyes for Annette. She was wearing a gray coat, a red knit dress, red gloves and gray shoes, and she looked stunning. I managed to squeak out "Hello" in a very happy but nervous voice, and she said "Hello" in her familiar low but sweet voice.

We had lunch at the Sheraton along with one of the local movie managers and Annette's mom, Virginia, who was just as charming as Annette. She was like any other mother, too. Annette told me about all of her stuffed animals and the names of each one. She also talked about her family, including relatives still in New York. She gave me an autographed photo, then wrote this in my autograph book: "To Janet, It was so nice meeting you today and congratulations on winning the contest. Love, Annette." What a thrill!

The rest of that wonderful day was spent mostly in public. Many people recognized her and asked for her autograph, and she took time to sign every single one. Unfortunately, we didn't get to see *Babes in Toyland*, but I knew I could always catch it later.

Being introduced to a star you've admired since you were five years old is really the end! I was amazed at how pleasant she was to talk to and how she kept us at ease. For this young fan, meeting Annette was like a dream—one that came true!

Janet Almanzi Lundy was lucky enough to win a meeting and lunch with Annette in New York, 1961.

Karen Pendleton

Mouseketeer

The tiniest Mouseketeer on the Red Team was Karen Pendleton, who was only 9 when the show began. She was a good dancer and singer, often paired in duets with short-term Mouse Johnny Crawford and, of course, Cubby O'Brien. Karen had an adorable, raspy singing voice, long golden curls and an irresistible grin. She appealed to audiences of all ages, and received a great deal of fan mail. She was given her own mini-series, both narrating and starring in "Karen in Kartoonland," a feature that explained how animation worked. She also narrated the popular "Annette" series.

After the *MMC* ended, Karen dropped out of show business and worked at various jobs. She married in 1970 and had a daughter in 1973, but the marriage sadly ended in divorce.

Karen turned her attention to college, earning a B.A., followed by a Master of Science degree in Psychology. Misfortune struck in 1983, when an automobile accident left her paralyzed from the waist down. Always a trouper, she continued to attend post-*MMC* events in a wheelchair. Being younger than Annette and most of the other Mouseketeers, Karen mostly hung out with Cubby. It wasn't until several years later that she and Annette got to know each other and became close friends.

"The other Mouseketeers were four years older than Cubby and me, so we were always together. We are friends even to this day. After the show ended, Annette and I didn't have much contact, but Sharon and I remained close," Karen recalls.

Bonding with Annette came in 1980, during the *Mickey Mouse Club's* 25th anniversary reunion show on TV.

"Annette and I became closer during the reunion show," says Karen. "She told me things about her that I didn't know. I didn't remember this, but she said she loved that she could sit with me and brush my hair—she always wanted long hair and never did have it till she got older.

"She was so accepting of people, and we got along great. Later on, when we both had disabilities, she and I got closer because we could talk about our problems and how it changed our lives."

Karen fondly remembers narrating the MMC's popular "Annette" series.

"It was fun narrating it, but I wanted to be IN it! But I was too little. After Annette, Cubby and I got the most fan mail. Everyone likes little tiny kids. I still get fan mail today, but they're from 40-year-olds," she says with a chuckle.

Mouseketeers Cheryl Holdridge and Karen Pendleton sing with Annette in their Talent Roundup outfits on the *MMC*. (Photo © The Walt Disney Company)

One of her memories includes the little Mouseketeer romances that took place behind the scenes, noting that "All the boys loved Annette."

"There's so much that we did offscreen—tons of stories—mostly about how the older kids tried to fight for the love of each other. Annette was with Lonnie, then Sharon was with Lonnie, then Sharon was with Tommy.

And it was Cubby and Karen all the time, just not romantically! Cubby was adorable."

When the show ended, so did Karen's performing career.

"After the *Mickey Mouse Club*, most of the cast went to the Hollywood Professional School. I went to regular school because my parents wanted me to be a normal kid. I was extremely insecure, but my (1983) accident gave me confidence," she recalls. "It's all in the attitude. My daughter needed me, so I took care of her through high school. Then my parents got sick in 2004, so I quit my job and took care of them."

Her parents passed away in 2006. Not long afterward, Karen herself came close to dying from an illness related to her paralysis. In 2004, Karen appeared with several other Mouseketeers on the Walt Disney Treasures DVDs interview, conducted by noted film critic Leonard Maltin. In 2005, she took part in the 50th Anniversary Celebration for the *Mickey Mouse Club*. She received a Disney Legend Award from the Disneyana Fan Club in 2014.

Sadly, Karen passed away on Oct. 6, 2019, at age 73.

Ed Held

Louisiana Fan Club President

When I first saw the *Mickey Mouse Club* as a kid, my eye always went directly to Annette! Seeing a popular Italian girl on TV meant a lot to me and the other not-so-popular Italians in my New Orleans neighborhood. Later in high school, I awoke one day and the radio was blasting "Tall Paul." The voice sounded familiar, and when the DJ said it was Mouseketeer Annette, the joy that song made me feel was tremendous. I bought the record, and later collected the rest of her albums and singles.

At that point, I had become a big fan and joined Rita Vandeveer's Annette Fan Club. A few years later, I met Rita while on a business trip to Indianapolis and asked her if I should start a fan club for Annette in New Orleans. She said of course! I got a lot of members by listing my club in teen magazines.

Around 1967 I had an opportunity to go to California and Rita gave me Annette's contact information. I first went to see her dad, Joe, at his service station, and showed him all of the Annette publicity pictures I had brought. He responded, "You have more pictures of my daughter than I do!" Then I called Annette's mom, Virginia, and we set a date and time for me to visit at her parents' home. I wore a suit out of respect for Annette and brought her a bouquet of flowers.

Annette showed up with Gina, who was a toddler, and we had a nice chat. We took pictures and movies (unfortunately, all were destroyed by Hurricane Katrina) and Annette signed about 20 photos for my fan club members. Annette loved her fans and never hesitated to give autographs or provide photos for her fan clubs.

Several years passed: Annette was raising her family and I got a degree in Fine Art. Then, in 1985, I heard Annette was coming to the French Quarter to be the Grand Marshal for our annual St. Joseph Italian-American Parade. Her friend Kathy Maraldo *(Editor's note: See Kathy's story elsewhere in this book)*, whose family was involved in the Italian-American Marching Club, invited me to join a small group and meet Annette at the New Orleans Airport.

We were put in a private room where I chatted with Annette about the hundreds of red, green and silver doubloon-type plastic coins with her image on them that she would toss into the crowd as she rode along the parade route. Those turned into collector's items very quickly! Even in the middle of such a busy time, Annette was so sweet to me and signed my *Italiannette* album.

Later we all went to the legendary Court Of Two Sisters restaurant where we posed for photos. I have a special photo of Annette sitting on a chair in the courtyard and it is priceless. Annette ordered a Vodka Seven on the rocks and relaxed for a bit, then went to meet families with kids and have photos

Ed Held was a fan club president who enjoyed helping Annette during her visits to New Orleans in the 1980s. (Photo: Edward J. Held Collection)

taken. Even during her down time, she was gracious enough to meet fans and pose for pictures with them.

For her parade introduction, I gave the DJ her "Beach Party" song, which she had approved beforehand. Then, during the parade, as Annette was riding in a convertible, some kids wanted to get an autograph. She had nothing to write on so I gave them some wallet-size photos for her to sign. She asked the kids where they got the photos and they pointed at me. Annette shouted "Thank you!" and later signed a photo for me that said, "Eddie, many thanks for all your good work!" It was a lot of fun being part of Annette's first trip to the Big Easy!

In 1993, a year after she went public with her MS, Annette returned to New Orleans with her parents to be Grand Marshal in the parade. She also appeared on a local afternoon TV show hosted by Angela Hill, who wore Mickey Mouse Ears and gave a pair to each audience member. They really loved it! I provided the show with some photos and other information.

When I went backstage to talk to Annette, Virginia and Joe, Annette had that famous acrylic cane with hand-painted Disney characters on it that the Disney Studio had given to her. She let me hold it and—wow—what beautiful art work! Before the TV taping, I was asked to sing the *Mickey Mouse Club Alma Mater* before Annette appeared on camera. I was in the show for a second as I sat to the side of the stage with Virginia and Joe.

Later in 1993, I met Annette and Glen at Walt Disney World where she was going to sell her Cello perfume and sign the boxes. I took photos of them as they walked out of the Floridian Hotel and she was walking very slowly with her Disney cane. It was heartbreaking.

Although the hurricane washed away a lot of my photos and memorabilia, I still have Annette's music and play it regularly thanks to a friend who recorded all of her LPs for me. I keep in touch with her family and donate to Annette's fund for neurological diseases, so her memory is very much in my life. My dream of meeting Annette was fulfilled and I thank God that it took place when the world was solid and she was everyone's Pineapple Princess!

Donna Loren

Singer

Singer Donna Loren has a couple of connections to Annette, starting with her appearance on the *Mickey Mouse Club's* Talent Round-Up Day. On March 7, 1957, Donna got her "ears" for singing "I Didn't Know the Gun was Loaded" and "Pennies from Heaven." Years later, as a cast member in several of American International Pictures' beach movies, she again met up with Annette in four of them. While her main role was as a singer, she had a few lines and spent time with Annette between scenes.

Donna recalls her *Mickey Mouse Club* appearance with fondness:

"Annette was someone I could look up to! Literally!" she says with enthusiasm. "On my tenth birthday, I performed under the direction of Sidney Miller on the *Mickey Mouse Club*. Annette, Doreen and Cheryl joined me in affirming 'no rain,' holding umbrellas upside-down while I sang 'Pennies from Heaven.' Annette was a whole head taller than me, looking from above with loving eyes and a friendly grin. Sure eased a little girl's nerves and made me feel welcome."

Seven years later, Donna and Annette looked eye-to-eye at AIP and had one unusual thing in common: covered-up navels. From 1963 to 1968, Donna was "the Dr Pepper Girl," and as such had to coordinate other appearances with that company. Singing on *Shindig*, where she was a featured vocalist, was no problem, but the beach movies presented a conflict.

"I was the Dr Pepper Girl and thrust into selling the product in *Muscle Beach Party*, singing a duet with the king of surf guitar, Dick Dale. The song was co-written by Brian Wilson, whose production and background vocals were featured in the movie as well as my single, 'Muscle Bustle.' One day, Annette and I were informed that although all the 'beach bunnies' were bikini clad, she and I were contractually bound to never expose our navels! She from Disney, mine dictated by Dr Pepper!"

Donna says that the wholesome image she and Annette shared were "a trait that we genuinely portrayed. Of course, another shared experience was a certain appeal we had that never betrayed our faithfulness to our gender. Annette and I were all girl! In fact, that was our strength."

Donna still writes songs and performs. Her first book, *Pop Sixties: Shindig!, Dick Clark, Beach Party, and Photographs from the Donna Loren Archive*, was released in 2017.

Singer Donna Loren met Annette as a guest on the *Mickey Mouse Club*, then appeared with her in the movie *Pajama Party* for AIP in 1964. (Photo: American International Pictures)

Jeff Johnson

California Fan

Looking at old pictures, I found several that my mom took of me sitting in a rocking chair, watching the *Mickey Mouse Club*. I was a toddler and it made her happy that I was occupied for a whole hour. I developed a crush on Annette then, and she became an important part of my life. She brought me so many great memories through her music, movies and TV appearances. To actually meet her and spend time with her like I later did was too crazy!

In 1988, a friend who knew Annette invited me to join her on a short road trip from San Diego, with the unbelievable goal of actually meeting my idol and her mom. We got to a Beverly Hills restaurant early, and I was so nervous as we waited with another fan who had also been invited to lunch. When Annette walked in, my face was beet red! I gave her a long-stemmed red rose and we shook hands. Inside the restaurant, she sat across from me so I could see her well, and I marveled over the fact that this was happening. She said she was going to pay for our lunches and to order what we wanted. All of the ladies were having salads and I had a burger and fries!

We talked for quite a while, and after lunch we walked outside where she turned to us and said, "Come with me to drop Mom off." No hesitation on my part!

We drove to her parents' house in Encino, where a palm tree in the front yard caught my attention. I told Annette I remembered her taking a publicity photo there wearing a gold blouse in 1984 or '85. She asked if I'd like to see the house, and of course I said sure! One of the things I immediately noticed was the painting of Annette that was on the cover of the *Something Borrowed, Something Blue* album, hanging in the living room over the couch. Virginia told me how much she loved that painting.

Then we went into Annette's old bedroom—the one I had seen so many times in movie magazines. Was I actually standing there?! I asked Annette if we could take pictures of her famous round bed and she said sure! She sat on the bed and grabbed her big stuffed tiger—a gift from Fabian—for the photo. We stayed in the bedroom for an hour or so, talking about many things. She was so welcoming and always smiling. I was so nervous because this was such a big day in my life, but she made me feel comfortable.

Then something incredible happened: She said her mom had things to do, so how would we like to go to her own home? Wow! We spent the rest of the day there and got the royal treatment. She gave us something to drink and we took photos in all of the rooms. When we went into the kitchen, I put a few pieces from my collection on the table that I hoped she would autograph. She said, "Do you want me to sign these? No problem!" Then she went into a cabinet and brought out envelopes and photos, and said "How about one of these?" She gave me a new photo plus signed my stuff, which amounted to about 10 things. She kept saying it was no problem at all. "I get stacks of mail, so I have all those to sign too. People send me postage and I just have to sign them."

It was such a remarkable day, and about 6 p.m. we headed back to San Diego. Annette had been sweet and accommodating, and showed a lot of genuine interest in our lives. I couldn't believe that what started out as lunch turned into a whole day with her!

During the next few years, I saw Annette several times. There were her concerts with Frankie at the Orange County Fair and Knott's Berry Farm, where we got to go backstage; cheering her on when she got her star on the Hollywood Boulevard Walk of Fame; and an appearance for her teddy bear company at Disneyland.

When she got her star on the Walk of Fame in 1993, she was just beaming as she stepped out of the limo. She looked thrilled and overwhelmed with the photographers all over her! There

Jeff Johnson, a fan club vice-president, was another admirer who
enjoyed a friendship with Annette. (1991 photo: Nick Strange)

were several of us fan/friends there, and Annette invited us
back to her house for a luncheon after the event. Her mom and
dad were there, and Frankie Avalon showed up with a big roll of
posters. Annette looked at him like, what have you gotten me
into now? He said, "Don't worry, they're all for charity." They
turned out to be reproductions of *Beach Party* posters—100 of
them—for her to sign. He had already autographed them all,
and later she took the time to sign every single one.

There also were playful moments with Annette. Once I had
lunch with her and Glen, and on the way home Annette sug-
gested we stop at Baskin Robbins for ice cream. Glen pulled in
to the shop and Annette and I headed into the store. A young
guy working there recognized her immediately and got very
nervous as we approached the counter. We were focused on
the menu sign above his head, trying to decide what flavors to
have, and we talked about all the flavors we loved. I settled on
butter pecan and Annette chose pistachio, her favorite.

I reached into my pocket and pulled out my wallet, saying
"My treat!" Annette answered, "Oh no, it's my treat!" and we
went back and forth, each of us insisting on paying. I explained
that she paid for lunch so I'd get the ice cream. She insisted that

I could get the bill next time. I said, "It's a date!" We arrived back at the car with ice cream and big smiles on our faces.

My fun memories of Annette are plentiful, but what I remember most is her compassion. When my mom became ill with Parkinson's, Annette called me every Monday at noon, like clockwork, to check on Mom and see how I was doing. Annette had MS at this time and but never mentioned it. Her only concern was my mom. The phone calls went on for months until Mom passed away.

Later, when I took my family to her teddy bear show at Disneyland, Annette hugged me and held on to me and said she was so sorry. There were tears running down her face. She asked how I was, and was so happy that I had brought my wife and kids with me. She encouraged my three kids—all under the age of 10—to "go on the rides and have fun all day." Then she gave me an extra hug before we left her.

Her concern for my mom showed me how Annette cared so much for people, always putting others before herself. She always treated me like I was close family. I was one lucky guy to know Annette Funicello.

Arlene Sullivan

American Bandstand Dancer

The friendship between Annette and Arlene Sullivan began as a shared joke, one that Arlene recalls with a laugh many years later.

Arlene was a popular dancer paired with Kenny Rossi on *American Bandstand*, Dick Clark's Philadelphia music and dance show that teenagers rushed home from school to watch. Not only could you hear the newest rock 'n' roll tunes and learn the latest dance moves, you also could see your favorite singers make guest appearances on the show. In 1960, Annette went to Philly to promote her latest record, *O Dio Mio*, and met Arlene.

"She came right up to me and said, 'I get a lot of letters saying that I look like you,' and I told her that I'd get letters saying I looked like her! We'd laugh about it," Arlene recalls. It was an instant friendship.

"I immediately liked her. We started to talk, and she asked for my address and phone number. After she went back to the West Coast I'd get a letter from her once a week. We'd write to each other all the time. When she came to New York for an appearance in 1961, her mom called my mom to ask if it would be OK if I spent the week with her, that it would be nice to have someone to keep her company. My parents took me to the train station, then I went to the hotel in New York and Annette and I spent a week together," she says.

"I had watched her on the *Mickey Mouse Club* like everyone else. Spending time with her was such a treat for me!"

The first weekend Annette was in New York she appeared four times a day at Radio City Music Hall with singer Dick Roman, whose popular songs were "Theme from A Summer Place" and "Touch of Love." Annette's chart hits at the time were her Sherman Brothers tunes "Pineapple Princess" and "Dream Boy," the latter from her *Italiannette* album. Arlene tagged along to watch the show from backstage and recalls that Annette and Dick sang a couple of duets.

"There I was, backstage meeting the Rockettes, and they said they used to watch me on *Bandstand*," she says. "They were treating me like I was a celebrity and I'm meeting the ROCKETTES! I was so excited to see them."

Arlene is among Annette's many friends who appreciated her sense of humor, which emerged during her Radio City appearance. Annette and Dick drove onto the stage in a convertible, and before the second show Annette took Arlene aside with a plan. "She said to me, 'Get in the back seat and lie on the floor when we go out onstage! It would be our secret!' I said don't you think the people in balcony would see me? We laughed because she hadn't thought about that."

The next night Frankie Avalon was in town and he came to the hotel to see Annette and take her on a carriage ride in Central Park. Arlene says, "I stayed with her mom and they went off together. When she came back I saw lipstick

American Bandstand regular Arlene Sullivan was an Annette lookalike who met her when she appeared on the show. They remained friends for many years.

smeared on his face! He stayed for a while, then we started to get silly. We had a good time. We had fun being silly together."

During their times together Annette would call her best friend, actress Shelley Fabares, and introduce her to Arlene over the phone. "Shelley was so, so nice to me," she remembers.

During her week in New York Arlene and Annette would stay up all night talking about boys. "She'd talk about Frankie and Fabian...I knew these guys from Philly and I really liked them. Annette said, 'There's only one I really REALLY like and that's Paul Anka.' I said, 'you're kidding,' and she said 'he's the one.' I told her I could see the attraction—he's so romantic with his songs. I had conversations with her mom about Paul and her mom wasn't that crazy about him because he had other girlfriends."

Even as part of the Philly scene, Arlene knew she couldn't get involved with any of the popular teen singers. "Once I was in a dressing room with Paul Anka, and when he walked me to the door he tried to kiss me. I was so startled I said, 'Oh, I like your shirt!' So he took it off and gave it to me!" she recalls with a laugh.

Arlene says she never visited Annette in California, but whenever her friend came East they would get together. As they got older, Annette and Arlene lost touch, which Arlene regrets to this day. "She had gotten married and I went on with my life," she says. "I moved several times over the years but always kept Annette's letters.

"In 1994 Annette was on the *Sally Jessy Raphael Show* but I didn't know about it. Later, after I moved, I found a letter from someone who said Annette had wanted to get in touch with me. Someone attending the show was wearing a T-shirt with a photo of me and Annette on it, and they asked someone working with Annette for her number to put us in touch. She said she couldn't give it out."

Despite that disappointment, Arlene shares great memories of Annette in her book, *Bandstand Diaries: The Philadelphia Years, 1956-1963*, a nostalgic look at the fashions, the fads, the dance steps and whatever happened to the regulars who danced on the show. She even shares some of Annette's letters to her.

"I have never met a person as sweet as Annette Funicello," says Arlene. "There's no celebrity who could ever meet her standards. She was the best!"

Lonnie Burr

Mouseketeer

As a child actor, singer and dancer, Lonnie Burr had a lot of experience under his belt before signing on to the *Mickey Mouse Club*. He had performed on TV, stage and radio as well as in movies and commercials prior to becoming a Red Team Mouseketeer. When the show ended, he continued as a director, performer and choreographer, then discovered he had a talent for writing while working on his Ph.D in English Literature. In 1985, he appeared with Annette and Martin Mull in a Disney Channel movie, *Lots of Luck*.

Beyond his talent as a Mouseketeer, Lonnie is known for being Annette's first boyfriend—and giving her her first kiss.

"We fell in love soon after we all got together in 1955," Lonnie recalls. "I had not known that I gave her her first kiss until I read her autobiography. We stayed together, like holding hands and a little making out, particularly on the long rides back from the Disneyland Circus at the Park at night, after performing in the Mickey Mouse Club Circus behind Fantasyland. We sang and danced there after we had the first year of the TV series completed.

"I asked Annie to go steady with me a few months after we fell together; I had a ring and gold chain and she took it. We were at a *MMC* party with kids and parents in someone's home. Annie showed it to her girlfriends and Doreen and the girls began running around and giggling and making a lot of noise. After her dad talked to Annie, he made her return the ring."

Like most young romances, it didn't last.

"Annette and I parted Jan. 10, 1956, when we took hiatus from the show. I had turned 12 on May 31, 1955, and Annie turned 13 in October. I liked older women! This is a very long time for a romance between kids in any era," says Lonnie. "Our early love was special. She was fun to be around even when we were working on other things."

It wasn't the last time they had a romantic encounter, though. As older teens, they ran into each other at a party at Doreen Tracey Washburn's house. The first Mouse to get married and have a baby, Doreen tied the knot with Bob Washburn in 1961, a marriage which lasted only a year. Several of the Mouseketeers attended the party, at which Doreen's mom, Bess, served as hostess.

While a couple of the Mice sang for the guests, Annette and Lonnie had other ideas about having a good time. They began flirting, which led to more.

"I think we scandalized Bess when she discovered Annette and I on the floor, making out," says Lonnie. "She was flustered and asked us to stop, so we did. After she left, we moved to another room. Annette was a lovely kissing partner!

"Then there was an embarrassing moment after the party when I followed Sharon (Baird) and Annie to Annie's house in Encino, to make sure they got home safely. When I walked them to the door we were met by Annette's mom, Virginia. After we greeted each other, she pointed to my neck and asked about the mark

Mouseketeers Lonnie Burr and Annette sign autographs. Lonnie gave Annette her first kiss! (Photo: Dorothy Burr, © Lonnie Burr)

that was on it. Apparently Annette had given me a hickey. When I told Virginia it was a birthmark, she said, 'Lonnie, I've known you since you were a young boy and you never had a birthmark!'"

Lonnie notes that although he and Annette didn't see each other regularly as adults, they would occasionally run into each other at Disneyland events and during Mouseketeer reunions on and off TV.

"We remained friends until she died. After she became ill, I would speak with her by phone until she could no longer accomplish that. Her husband, Glen, would tell me if Annette was having a good day or a bad day, and whether she would be up to hearing from me."

Lonnie is no stranger to MS: His mother and his tap and jazz teacher, Dee Blacker, also had the disease.

"The last time I saw Annette was when my wife Diane and I dropped by to see them when I was in L.A. for a commercial," Lonnie recalls. "Her state was very bad by then. Although I did not show it, I was very sad about her situation and that I could do NOTHING to help other than just being there. Glen was as true as he could be to her and stuck with her after the MS struck. He gave her great care and protection."

Lonnie admits that, while Annette was cute and "a swell kisser," his attraction went beyond that.

"She was pretty, of course. But she also had charisma. That's an overused noun but one that does exist. When Annette was on camera or performing, or even when she just entered a room at a party or for whatever reason, she had charisma."

Lonnie continues to perform and has written two books of poetry, the non-fiction book *Two for the Show: Great 20th Century Comedy Teams* (iUniverse, 2000), the book and lyrics for the musical *Fantasies*, and his autobiography, *The Accidental Mouseketeer: Before and After the Mickey Mouse Club* (Theme Park Press, 2014).

Jodie Mann

California Fan

As a child growing up in New York, I was a typical fan when the Mouseketeers came into my home. So many of us that age watched the *Mickey Mouse Club*, and like any adoring fan, I was drawn to Annette. I loved her because she was Italian, like me, and it was very rare at that time to see anyone on TV who kind of looked like the people in my family! I loved the whole show, and it was a big deal to watch it.

Eventually, we moved to California. When I was a freshman in high school, my mom got a job as a legal secretary at American International Pictures in Los Angeles, the studio that made the beach movies. We lived right around the corner, so AIP quickly became a hangout where I made friends with the receptionist and the people in the mailroom. We got to go to special premieres of all the beach movies, and I was able to meet some of the people who worked in production. I often went with studio drivers back and forth to the set to watch the filming—including the beach scenes.

During one of the indoor shots filmed on a soundstage, I was waiting outside for the red light to go off so I could enter when Annette walked up with one of the production people, who introduced us. After that I went to the set almost every day to watch them film and Annette always said hello.

One particular day, her purple T-bird was sitting outside the door, and since it was always my favorite car I was drooling over it when Annette came outside. Someone told her the car had to be moved because they were going to need the space for a truck. I said something goofy about the car and she said,

"Do you have your license?" I was shocked when she handed me the keys and said I could drive it to her parking spot. (I was tempted to drive it right off the lot and home, but that was only a fleeting thought!)

When I returned her keys, she was sitting in her chair waiting for the next shot. She asked me to sit next to her in Frankie's seat, then made a funny comment about how he was a kind Italian and wouldn't mind me taking his chair. I immediately told her I was Italian, too, and we wound up talking about Italian families for quite a while.

She was always so nice to me. The crew took notice, and they all started asking me if I was coming back the next day. As an aspiring young actress, it was wonderful to be on the set and to see how movies were made. Deke Heyward, a scriptwriter at AIP, said that if he had known I wanted to be an actress he would have written in a part for me as Annette's little sister!

Once I went back to school, I didn't go to the set as much, but it was during that time the head of the AIP mailroom asked if I wanted to help him after school. I was given the assignment of answering Annette's fan mail, which meant opening the mail, reading and separating anything important I thought she should handle personally. For many fans, I'd put photos with Annette's pre-stamped signature into envelopes and address them back to the senders.

One day Annette was at the studio and happened to pass the mailroom. She came in and remarked how she wished she could answer them all, but it was impossible. I told her not to worry, that I had answered all the personal questions for her! She knew immediately I was kidding, and when she left she told them that they should give me a raise. That became a joke between all of us since I didn't get paid, but they did all chip in and get me a great gift (now I can't remember what that was!) I almost did go to work there part-time after school, but mom decided she wanted me to concentrate on my studies.

After I graduated from high school, Mom and I left California to go back to New York. Mom was transferred to the New York AIP office, so we were able to stay in touch with some of the West Coast people, but once I left California it was never really the same. However, I have wonderful memories of Annette and the whole AIP gang.

Years later, I moved back to California and was part of starting the Actors and Others for Animals organization, working with the likes of Doris Day (whom I idolized) and Lucille Ball. Someone came to work for us who was from back East, and I learned the woman was the head of Frankie Avalon's fan club all the years he was doing the beach movies. It's definitely a small world.

(Jodie went on to study acting and worked in theater, TV commercials and several TV series. She continued to produce fundraisers for Actors and Others for Animals and currently is an advocate for animal rescue groups in Southern California.)

Bobby Rydell

Singer

Everyone who followed the 1960s Teen Idols knows Bobby Rydell, the singer who emerged from Philadelphia along with his buddies, Frankie Avalon and Fabian. His hit songs include "Volare," "Wild One" and "We Got Love," among many others, and he appeared in the 1963 movie *Bye Bye Birdie*. While never romantically involved with Annette, Bobby has fond memories of their "publicity dates."

"The first time I went to California to do interviews and TV, back in 1960, Annette was my first date," he recalls. "Back then it was just a set-up date for publicity with the photos published in fan magazines. We didn't date privately at all, just did publicity dates and took photos, like the one of us with the drum set. Then I got to know her better and we became close. We just became very good friends."

In 1962, Annette and Bobby appeared in an episode of *Walt Disney's Wonderful World of Color*. Titled "Disneyland After Dark," and later released overseas as a theatrical short subject, it offered a view of Disneyland's nighttime entertainment, fireworks and celebrity guests. Others on the show were The Osmond Brothers, Louis Armstrong and Mouseketeer Bobby Burgess. Annette sang "Dance Annette" and Bobby Rydell performed "Around the World."

"I really didn't go to California that much since I lived in Philly, but I returned to do 'Disneyland After Dark,' which was a lot of fun. Annette was a sweetheart, just fantastic," says Bobby.

The singer shares a story from 1993, when Annette was honored with the Helen Hayes Award for Lifetime Achievement in New York. "Frankie was supposed to be there as a special

Singer Bobby Rydell and Annette on a
date in 1960. They were good friends
and not involved romantically.

guest for Annette, then he called me and said, 'Do me a favor. I can't be there, can you fill in for me?' I said absolutely!" says Bobby.

"I went to the theater in New York City and Annette was in the front row in a wheelchair. She looked fantastic. I did maybe 20 minutes to a half hour of songs, and one of the numbers I did was 'One Special Girl' from *Bye Bye Birdie*, which I sang to her. Then I came down and sat with Annette for the rest of the show. She said, 'Bobby, I don't understand, why are these people making such a fuss?' I said, 'My god, Annette, you're America's Sweetheart, for crying out loud!'"

In 1985, Bobby, Frankie and Fabian formed The Golden Boys of Bandstand touring show, which features their hit songs and other oldies. They perform one-nighters at casinos, festivals and smaller music venues. When Frankie left the trio in 1986 to make *Back to the Beach* with Annette, Chubby Checker took his place on the road.

"Frankie said that when they were making the movie Annette was a little unstable in walking, but she still looked like the beautiful Annette," says Bobby. "She was adorable and sweet; just a wonderful, wonderful lady."

The Golden Boys of Bandstand continue to tour and often do a tribute to Annette in their show.

Luree Nicholson / Salli Sachse

Beach Movie Actresses

Luree Nicholson

One of Annette's closest friends in adulthood was Luree Nicholson, who appeared with Annette in all of the American International Pictures beach movies produced by her father, James H. Nicholson. Married at the time, she was billed as Luree Holmes. She made the surf-n-sand flicks as a lark, later becoming a family counselor. She currently is a certified hypnotherapist in Los Angeles, specializing in medical and childbirth hypnosis. Luree, the mother of five, is the author of *How to Fight Fair with Your Kids and Win* (Wellness Institute, 2000).

Luree remembers the beach movie days as a lot of fun. Her friendship with Annette blossomed because they were misfits among the bikini crowd.

"We hit it off because she and I were the most conservative girls there, even down to our bathing suits," she says. "The biggest thing about our friendship was that we didn't fit in with the crowd. Everybody was very nice and we had a lot of fun. But we were different. I was in the movie business because my father was a producer. We had lots of down time during filming, sitting on the beach in 40-degree weather."

When Annette was sent to Europe to promote the beach movies, Luree was her traveling companion.

"It was the first time her mom hadn't gone with her on a tour," Luree recalls. "We were there around two weeks and it was the most fun thing we ever did. We were the same age, at 20, but I already had two kids. I had more life experience, but not that much more!"

With a lower drinking age in Europe, Annette and Luree were able to test their freedom with adult beverages. "This was the first time Annette was free to do as she pleased, and she was a little wild," Luree says with a laugh. "She wanted to party. We both found out that sweet drinks made us sick. Not throwing-up sick, but a little dizzy. After we got home and told her mom, Virginia, that we had had a few drinks, she said to me, 'You corrupted my daughter!' And I said 'No, it's the other way around! SHE encouraged ME!' We had a big laugh over it."

Luree said that when they hung out, Annette didn't talk much about boys. "She did talk a bit about Frankie. But mostly we just had fun. One time we got our hair done by Vidal Sassoon when he was really big."

When Annette and Jack Gilardi got married in 1965, Luree was one of her seven bridesmaids. Nine months later, when the Gilardis' daughter was born, Annette named her Gina Luree. "I was so surprised and honored," says Luree. "Annette said she always liked my name, and she didn't tell me she was going to do that beforehand."

Luree spent a lot of time with Annette after she was diagnosed with MS. "When she first got MS, initially she could sort of get around. But when she was not able to drive anymore I'd spend one day a week with her. We'd get our hair and nails done, have lunch, occasionally go to a doctor's appointment. It was just fun for her to get out."

One incident that stands out for Luree, the hypnotherapist, was during a visit when Annette had a bad cold. "She couldn't cough or swallow," Luree recalls. "I hypnotized her so she could relax her throat and take her medication."

Annette was always so patient, Luree says of their excursions. "She never complained about her MS, never got angry, always smiled and continued to be nice to everyone. She was an amazing friend."

Salli Sachse

Salli Sachse, one of the girls with waist-length hair in the beach movies, wasn't a close friend of Annette's but has fond memories of their beach movie days. Salli had an acting and modeling career for several years before going to Europe to study art. She now is a professional artist in La Jolla, Calif.

"I remember sitting around on the beach, waiting for our parts," Salli recalls. "The movies were shot in the winter for summer release. We were in our terry-cloth robes, sitting around the camp-fire, joking and freezing. One of the prop guys would pass around a bottle of brandy and we'd all take a swig. With

Actress-turned-painter Salli Sachse made several beach movies with Annette. This is a scene from *How to Stuff a Wild Bikini* in 1965. (Photo: American International Pictures)

Annette, one swig got her looped, and she got all giggly and silly. We also snickered about how silly the movie plots were."

Salli felt that, in some ways, Annette was very sheltered.

"She was close to her religion, she was vulnerable but very professional," says Salli. "She'd show up on time and know her words and songs. We were all pretty much in awe—she was so tiny and really packed a wallop.

"Annette was such a loving and kind person and very inno-cent in the ways of the world. She never had a bad thing to say about anyone."

Christopher Riordan

Actor, Singer, Dancer, and Choreographer

Christopher Riordan has an extensive Hollywood resume, having appeared in films such as *My Fair Lady* and *Raintree County* as well as roles in eight Elvis Presley films and specials. In 1962 he was handpicked by Fred Astaire to succeed him as dance partner for Barrie Chase in Las Vegas. Then, after several serious acting roles, he found himself on the beach yelling "Surf's up!" with Annette.

Annette, he says, helped to get him a better job.

"I adored her. I had always been a fan of hers so I was really excited to be working with her, although I wasn't thrilled about working on a beach movie," says Christopher. "I was 32 years old and they were all 18 and 19, and we were not as enthused about same things. I was raising my infant son by myself and accepted almost any job that came along.

"Originally I was one of the beach boys and danced in the sand, but the more I assisted the choreographer, the more he let me do. Then he was off to another studio, working on another picture. When the producers came down looking for him and found out he was working across the street, he got fired. That's when Annette said, 'Why not let Christopher do it? He's been doing it all along anyway.' I said, 'Are you sure? And she said, 'Of course.'"

Working with Annette was easy, Christopher discovered. "She did anything I asked her to do. On those films a lot of attractive actresses come in, like Diane McBain and Julie Parrish, and I never saw Annie act jealous or uppity. She was always a gracious hostess. She was gracious with everyone...I can't say enough nice things about her. She was so kind, no ego at all."

Annette's kindness extended to Tommy Kirk, her costar in *Pajama Party,* with whom she had worked with many times before in Disney films. At that time, Tommy was going through a rough period—he had a drug problem and had not yet come out as being gay, which later affected his career at Disney. According to Christopher, during filming of *Pajama Party* Tommy would spend hours in his dressing room, smoking pot. He didn't know his lines. "When Tommy couldn't remember his lines, Annie was totally patient with him," says Christopher.

When the beach movies had run their course, American International Pictures latched onto a new genre: stock car racing films. They kept Christopher on as choreographer for *Thunder Alley* and *Fireball 500,* the latter starring Annette, Frankie Avalon and Fabian. In *Fireball 500* a carnival scene features Annette singing and dancing to "Step Right Up." Christopher thought it could be improved.

"The dance moves were kind of bland, so I had the idea of giving her a scarf to play with," he recalls. In the scene, she drapes the scarf over her shoulder, swings it, then takes scarves from the backup singers and tosses them into the audience. "I gave her a prop that helped her identify with her character and made her more appealing. When she saw the number, she hugged me and said 'Thank you, you gave me some sex appeal.' Later, on her way back to her dressing room, she passed by me, pinched my arm, and with her eyes she seemed to be throwing me the biggest kiss. We were all on a wonderful high that morning.

"Annette was always prepared. I'd show her a dance routine, she'd come back the next day and she'd have it. A few tweaks and we were done. She took direction perfectly and communicated very well. She was a joy to work with."

Christopher says he was close to Guy Hemric, who wrote the music for the AIP films and occasionally appeared on screen in cameo roles.

"He had a lot of respect for Annette," Christopher recalls. "But one time she got me in trouble! We were doing *Fireball 500* and I showed Guy a number I had choreographed for Frankie and Fabian, and as a joke I made Frankie's part look ridiculous. He said to show it to Annie, that she'd get a kick out of it. When I showed it to her she laughed hysterically and said to show it to Frankie and Fabian just the way I had done it. Frankie took offense and he hasn't spoken to me since."

Annette also had a great sense of humor, which once caught Christopher offguard. "One day I knocked on her dressing room door. She asked who it was and said to come on in. She was pouring vodka into a glass of orange juice and I guess I looked like I was in shock. She said, 'What's the matter, haven't you ever seen a Mouseketeer have a screwdriver before?'"

The last time Christopher saw Annette was the early '90s when he went to a restaurant with friends after a dance award ceremony.

"Someone said, 'Oh, Christopher, there's a friend of yours sitting over there,' and when I looked across the room it was Annette and her family. She was acting a little strangely and someone said she was drunk. She was having a hard time getting out of her chair and going to the door. I didn't want to bother her, so I didn't go over to say hello. Later, we learned about the MS."

Christopher has written an as-yet-unpublished book about his experiences in Hollywood. He is in his 80s and still working.

Patricia Conklin

California Fan

Annette was my generation's sweetheart.

Growing up in the San Fernando Valley in the 1950s, there were many children around my age on my block, and I watched the *Mickey Mouse Club* with several neighborhood girls. Her roles in Disney's "Annette" and "Spin and Marty" series epitomized my youthful fantasy of a best friend. I especially related to her because her character often seemed to be misunderstood, yet she handled herself with grace and poise. She was my model for how to "be." Her character was always nice, always kind. Always.

I would have loved to run into Annette on the street. As time went by, many friends reported having seen her around the San Fernando Valley, at a family amusement park in Burbank, in Toluca Lake shops, or in the new outdoor shopping centers where there were popular department stores. Later she was seen at various restaurants and civic events all around the Valley and Greater Los Angeles. There was always a hope in the back of my mind that one day I'd catch a glimpse of her.

Then, in 1975, when I was a newly-divorced mom working in a somewhat "trendy" and always-packed restaurant in Northridge, I answered the phone to hear a very soft and polite voice say she would like to make a takeout order. I knew before she said her name that I was interacting with Annette! I hoped that I would behave in a professional manner when she arrived—I didn't want to "gush."

When she walked into the restaurant 20-or-so minutes later, every head in the packed waiting area turned. She looked straight at me, walked up to me and said "Hi" with a genuine smile. She didn't look around the room, she didn't fluff her hair or do any other attention-grabbing things that other stars are often inclined to do when out in public. I told her it would be just a few minutes for her order and she stood right there with me, chatting about ordinary things. She was gracious, friendly, kind, approachable and totally unassuming. She was classy.

I've met and interacted with many people in show business, but few were as genuine as Annette—and none were as memorable.

Eileen Diamond Rogosin

Mouseketeer

A second-season replacement Mouseketeer, Eileen Diamond specialized in ballet and modern dance. Following her single season with the show, she joined regional theater in Southern California as a dancer, writer, choreographer, casting director and producer. During that time she met conductor-composer Roy M. Rogosin, whom she married in 1964. They have two adult children.

While she and Annette weren't close friends, Eileen fondly remembers her brief *MMC* days. "She was the nicest human being," Eileen says of Annette. "We didn't have time to get together as friends because we were busy working."

An accomplished dancer, Eileen says that when her dance teacher saw a video of Annette doing ballet, she wasn't impressed with her skills. "Annette wasn't the best of anything (on the show), but she was kind, congenial and lovely," Eileen remembers. "I really enjoyed knowing her at the time, and I thought her mom was very sweet."

A few years later, when Annette was filming *Babes in Toyland* at the Disney Studio, Eileen was hired to play one of the townspeople in the musical.

"I was 18 when I worked with her in *Babes*. Annette had just had new publicity photos taken, and we were going through all the photos and commenting on them. They were stunning! Her hair was lovely and pulled into a bow at her neck, and the costumes were magnificent in the film," says Eileen. "We just sat there talking and going over all of the photos and deciding which ones were the best. I was always deferential to her...I didn't want to invade her space."

Like others of Annette's friends and acquaintances, Eileen remembers her as truly the girl next door. "Annette didn't act like she was a big star. She couldn't understand how she got all the attention she did on the *Mickey Mouse Club*. She got more fan mail than we did, but we all got some. She was just like everyone else."

An aside: Eileen remembers when Annette's *Babes in Toyland* co-star, Tommy Sands, was dating Nancy Sinatra. "On her birthday he kept sneaking off the set to send her flowers every hour!" says Eileen. (They eventually married and divorced.)

Eileen and Roy live in Todos Santos on Baja Sur, Mexico, where they write musicals but no longer perform. She has written a memoir called *The Mouseketeer That Roared* that will be published in early 2020 by Theme Park Press.

Tommy Kirk

Actor

In the late 1950s, teenage Tommy Kirk emerged as a popular Disney actor after he was signed to play Joe Hardy in two "Hardy Boys" serials, based on the best-selling books by Franklin W. Dixon and aired on the *Mickey Mouse Club* before an enthusiastic young audience. His co-star was Tim Considine, soon to be equally popular with the teen set. Both boys went on to appear in Annette's first full-length movie, *The Shaggy Dog*, in 1959.

Tommy made four other feature films, as well as two made-for-TV movies, with Annette. At Disney, their performances in *Babes in Toyland* and the TV movies *Escapade in Florence* (released theatrically overseas) and *Horsemasters* delighted fans. Still at Disney, Tommy followed up with starring roles in *The Misadventures of Merlin Jones* and its sequel, *The Monkey's Uncle*. Annette played his girlfriend in both. Not long afterward, under the American International Pictures banner, they co-starred in *Pajama Party* and *How to Stuff a Wild Bikini*.

Tommy went on to make several low-budget B movies in the late '60s and early '70s, eventually leaving show business to run a successful carpet cleaning and upholstery business.

What he remembers most about Annette was her professionalism on the set. "She was a very disciplined actress, very controlled," he recalls. "She did not show a lot of emotion off-screen, unlike a lot of actresses who thrived on drama. She didn't need massaging."

Annette, he notes, was always prepared to work.

"She was very professional and her deportment was perfect. She never argued with a director and always knew her lines. People didn't swear around her and she never told a dirty joke.

Tommy Kirk made several movies with
Annette for both Disney and AIP. This is
a scene from *The Monkey's Uncle,* 1965.
(Photo © The Walt Disney Company)

She was very much a lady in the best, old-fashioned sense of the word. Annette focused on other people; she did not talk about herself with me or anyone else that I ever saw."

Tommy remembers one thing that sparked Annette's interest on the set: animals. "She loved animals and came unglued if someone brought a pet on the set," he says with a chuckle.

While they were not close friends in real life, Tommy and Annette enjoyed each other's company while filming, and their screen chemistry was evident. Tommy did become very close to Virginia Funicello, who always accompanied her young teen daughter on film assignments that required travel, including to Italy and London.

"I remember Annette had this big crush on (British pop singer) Cliff Richard when we were in London," says Tommy. "She was enamored of him and talked about him all the time!"

Tommy was inducted as a Disney Legend in 2006 and occasionally has appeared at autograph shows in recent years. He is now retired and lives in Las Vegas.

Ping Gee

Arizona Fan Club President

Along with the rest of the country, I started watching the *Mickey Mouse Club* in 1955. Immediately, Annette became my favorite Mouseketeer, and I continued to follow her career in fan magazines and movies.

When I was in junior high school, I found fan club listings in one of the movie magazines and joined two of them. One was headed by Rita Vandeveer (now Rose) and another by Bonnie Kirn (now Wendt), and I wrote to both, not realizing that this would be the start of lifelong friendships. I remember my first letter from Rita: The ink was purple and for a minute I thought I had received my own letter back because the handwriting was round, just like Annette's and my own! We became pen pals and tried to outdo each other, writing on toilet paper and cellophane!

I had always wanted to start a fan club for Annette. I wrote to her for permission and was thrilled when she agreed. Because she was so busy, most of my correspondence was with her mother, Virginia, but Annette was an active honoree and always appreciated her fans' support.

My father got me a mimeograph machine and I taught myself to cut stencils on our manual typewriter, and began producing newsletters and journals for my growing fan club. I took a graphic arts class in high school and used our family bathroom to print copies of photos for the journals. I didn't have an enlarger, so they were pretty teeny tiny prints, but the club members seemed to like them.

In 1964, just before my junior year in high school, my family decided to temporarily relocate from Tucson, Arizona to California. My parents leased their grocery store and our living quarters behind it, and we headed for Los Angeles. I was so excited to be closer to Annette!

Several letters between Virginia and me resulted in a dream come true when we finally settled on a time for me and my family to visit the Funicellos at their home in Encino. I remember my father and mother visiting with Annette's parents in the living room while my sister, Woo, and I waited for Annette to come home. I didn't realize that she was dropped off by Frankie Avalon, but my sister remembers! I wish I had seen that!

When Annette got home, she took me into her bedroom so we could chat. It was fantastic: There was the round bed that I had seen in the fan magazines, her piles of stuffed animals and the bottles of perfume she collected. I couldn't believe I was sitting there talking with Annette! I was in a daze and don't remember most of what we talked about, but I do remember that Annette was so gracious and sweet to me. She signed my autograph book and said she was glad to finally meet me.

Ping Thom Gee ran one of several Annette fan
clubs in the 1960s. (1973 photo: Rita Rose)

Later, I was thrilled when Virginia gave me a real treasure—one of Annette's own outfits, a white blouse with an orange jumper that had a large, single pocket in front. She joked that they called it Annette's kangaroo jumper.

I finally met Rita in 1969 after several years of correspondence, when my husband and I were in Indianapolis on business. Her purple Mustang made a big impression on me! I was able to connect with her AND Annette in 1973, when Rita and her husband were in L.A. and I was there with my sister. All four of us were invited to Annette's home. It was a fun visit with lots of photos being taken, and we got to meet Annette's children, Gina and Jacky. As always, Annette was a gracious hostess with an amazing talent to put visitors at ease.

In 2013, Rita and Bonnie flew to California to attend Annette's memorial at the Walt Disney Studios in Burbank and we were able to meet at a restaurant. It was a great visit over coffee and pie, with lots of Annette memories being shared.

One of the very special things about running a fan club for Annette was meeting so many nice people across the country. Without our fan club connections, we wouldn't have known each other all these years. We started out as teenage fans, and now we're in our 70s! We can thank Annette for opening her home to us, always being attentive to her fans, and for giving us such long-lasting friendships.

George Griner

Cinematographer

1955 was a magical year for me. The long anticipated opening of Disneyland took place in July and my grandmother took my sister, my brothers and me for the memorable event. And, at the ripe old age of seven, I fell in love.

The original *Mickey Mouse Club* started that year and every boy in America from ages of 7 to 15 was mesmerized by the beautiful 12-year-old Mouseketeer, Annette Funicello. None more so than yours truly. Fast forward 30 years to 1985. I found myself as first assistant camera on a Disney television feature called *Lots of Luck* starring...Annette!

As a first AC, you work in close proximity with the talent. And in the film world, I have discovered over the years that there are actors and actresses that are down-to-earth, friendly, fun to work with and really understand the "team" concept of film production. There are others who place themselves on marble pillars, are narcissistic, unfriendly and difficult to work with. I so wanted Annette to be of the first category.

She didn't disappoint. On the first day of shooting, as I was getting focus marks, she walked over to me and said, "Hi, I'm Annette, and I'm so excited to be working with you on this project."

A few weeks earlier, at a Disney memorabilia store in Los Angeles, I had purchased a period Annette Funicello fan book and I asked if she would autograph it to my young daughter. She took it and the next day returned it to me, having filled an entire page! She told my daughter how lucky she was to have me as her dad and how much she was enjoying working with me.

I cherish the memories of working on a film with an amazing person and consummate professional such as Annette Funicello.

Sandy Ferra Martindale
Childhood Friend

Sandra "Sandy" Ferra was one of Annette's closest childhood friends. She is the daughter of Mary Lou and Tony Ferra, who were owners of The Crossbow Inn, Red Velvet and Rag Doll nightclubs in the San Fernando Valley, which often were frequented by Elvis Presley. Sandy dated Elvis for several years and appeared as a dancer in six of his movies. She later married game show host Wink Martindale.

But before that, starting in the early '50s, the Ferras formed a circle of close friends with Joe and Virginia Funicello and another couple, Dottie and Joe Pietroforte. When the Pietrofortes adopted son Louis, Annette was chosen to be his godmother. *(See Louis's story elsewhere in this book.)*

"Annette and I grew up together," says Sandy. "At Christmas we would go to their house to open presents and Annette and I would show each other what we got. We spent holidays together and her mother was my little sister Annette's godmother. Our families had a lot of parties together—Virgie and my mom were good Italian cooks."

Sandy remembers Annette as being quite bashful as a child. "Her parents would bring her to the Rag Doll Club as a young girl and she'd tap dance on her toes. She was very shy...her mother wanted her to dance and Annette was crying and didn't want to. But as she got older, she loved to dance. When I was going with Elvis he said he'd like to meet her sometime. I don't think they ever did."

After Annette became a Mouseketeer, Sandy relished the fun of going with her on hayrides and to parties with Doreen Tracey, Cheryl Holdridge and Tommy Cole (who later became the makeup artist for Wink on his game shows). And she was really excited to see Annette and the other Mouseketeers perform at Disneyland the day it opened.

"Walt Disney adored her," Sandy recalls. "After she started on the *Mickey Mouse Club*, it didn't change our relationship, but Annette spent less time with us. We always managed to see each other at a restaurant when we had dinner with our parents."

Growing up, Sandy's dad would have big birthday parties for her at the Rag Doll. "Lassie always performed," she says, "and Annette and her brother Joey were at all of them. Michael was born later. As teenagers, we spent a lot of time in my dad's nightclubs. We'd spend New Year's Eve together with Annette's girlfriend, Shelley Fabares, at The Crossbow nightclub, then we'd go to Dottie and Joe's house on New Year's Day. On one New Year's, Shelley said she forgot to eat, and I thought how can anyone forget to eat? We laughed about that, then we started eating nuts."

As they got older and Annette started dating Paul Anka, Sandy remembers them "being in a room arguing and having a lot of disagreements. They were not well-suited but they loved each other."

When Annette started filming the beach movies, she worked hard at keeping a slim figure, says Sandy. "She dieted five days a week, then on weekends she'd have a cocktail and have fun!"

Sandy and Annette remained friends throughout adulthood. Annette kept her MS diagnosis a secret from friends and family for five years, but for Sandy, there were a couple of hints that something was wrong.

"One day we were talking on phone and she was listening to (psychologist and talk radio host) Toni Grant, where people called in with their problems. I asked why she was listening to that show and she said, 'It makes me feel better to know others have problems, too.' I didn't know what she was referring to. Another time a man from Parker Brothers, who adored her, told me he'd love to meet Annette. When I asked when we could get together, she said, 'Oh, Glen's out of town and I need him to be with me.' I didn't understand that Glen needed to be there to hold her up.

"Later, she told me she wasn't telling everyone about the disease, and that she didn't want her father to know because she thought it would kill him."

When Sandy's dad, Tony, had a 75th birthday celebration, Annette and her dad came for the festivities. A few years later, Annette and Sandy saw each other at a Gene Autry event, and Annette was in a wheelchair.

"We were always happy to see each other," Sandy says of their longtime friendship. "She was very special to me."

Judy Harriet Richman

Mouseketeer

Judy Harriet was an eight-year veteran of show business when she and Annette auditioned on the same day for the *Mickey Mouse Club*. Annette was three months older, and they both got the job, though Judy was on the show for only one season. Assigned to the Blue Team, which got less camera time than the more visible Mouseketeers on the Red Team, Judy enjoyed her on- and off-camera moments and delivered her assignments with a big smile. Her singing ability bumped her up to the Red Team shortly before the end of the first season, but she was dropped from the show in 1956.

Still, she has good memories of her *MMC* year and becoming friends with Annette.

"We opened Disneyland together, and we loved being part of that," Judy recalls. "Art Linkletter, Ronald Reagan and Robert Cummings were the hosts of the big party at the park in 1955.

"I remember we did the show's Circus Day and she and I learned how to do the trapeze. There were red-and-white candy striped tents. We learned a lot for 12- and 13-year-olds!"

Annette and her family lived in Studio City, Calif., during the show, and later Judy and her family moved there. "Our mothers were often on the set together. We all got along and it was a lot of fun," Judy says, recalling many of their shared times.

Judy remembers Annette as being "very sweet and softspoken. She didn't have a harsh word for anybody. She was a great lady, a graceful, grateful lady."

Even now, years after the original *Mickey Mouse Club*, fans continue to write to Mouseketeers at the studio, mainly due to reruns of the show.

"I still get fan mail at this stage of life and I'm shocked!" she says with a laugh. "It makes me feel wonderful that people still want autographed pictures. The *MMC* was part of an American institution and we will forever be people they know."

After she left the *Mickey Mouse Club*, Judy continued her singing career. She and Annette each recorded the song *Tall Paul* in 1959. Judy's was released first, but the song later gave Annette her first hit record. The girls' lives continued to connect after Judy joined the General Artists Corp. theatrical agency, where Annette's first husband, Jack Gilardi, was her agent.

For the next several years, Judy had success as a recording artist and sang in a handful of movies. Her spectacular rendition of "The Night That Rock and Roll Died" was a highlight of the Bing Crosby-Debbie Reynolds film *Say One for Me*. She also found herself in demand as a singer for live performances on the teenage show circuit, at civic events and at military bases.

In 1964, Judy married Tony Richman and had two daughters. She took part in the Mouseketeer reunion at Disneyland in 1975 and in the television special for the *MMC*'s 25th Anniversary in 1980.

Randall Nakashima

Blogger

To celebrate the 50th anniversary of the Mickey Mouse Club, 10 original Mouseketeers returned to Disneyland on Oct. 3, 2005, to share their memories of the children's TV show. Because of her health, Annette was unable to attend. But Disney crafted a set of gold Mickey Mouse Ears for Annette. Randall Nakashima, a contributor to TheOriginalMMC.com, wrote about his June 2017 visit to photograph the Ears in Bakersfield, Calif., where Annette resided before she passed away.

Annette's 50th Anniversary Ears are on display at Buck Owens' Crystal Palace in Bakersfield and are autographed by the Mouseketeers appearing at the 50th Anniversary Show at Disneyland. Annette, it turns out, was a country music fan, and a regular at the Crystal Palace when Buck was still playing.

Randall took a side trip that proved even more of a thrill when he stopped for lunch at Benji's French Basque Restaurant. His recollection of that day is excerpted from his blog on TheOriginalMMC. com and reprinted with that website's permission:

The surprise of the day came before the Crystal Palace when I stopped for lunch prior to my appointment. I went to a Basque restaurant about six blocks from the Palace, and by sheer luck, I had stumbled upon Annette's favorite Bakersfield restaurant. I was talking to the woman tending bar in the lounge and she responded that this was Annette's favorite restaurant, and that she and her husband, Glen Holt, were regulars for dinner and family occasions. She referred me to the hostess, Stephanie Duhart, who in turn referred me to her uncle, Benji.

Bernard "Benji" Arduain is the owner and original chef of the restaurant. Benji is a white-haired man in his 70s. He has

been in operation since 1986 and originally started in a build-
ing closer to downtown. Annette had been a customer since
he was in his old location. He called her "my beautiful girl,"
and said she would always come visit him in his kitchen when
he was cooking and would never think of leaving without
saying goodbye.

For anyone unfamiliar with a Basque restaurant, guests are
traditionally served family-style at long tables with everyone
passing the serving dishes across the table. Modernly, family
service is offered only if ordered by all the guests at an individ-
ual table, with traditional service reserved for private parties,
events or occasions. Basque entrees are very homey, and are
usually served with soup, salad, wine and cheese.

I can see how family-style seating and service would appeal
to Annette, used to large Italian family gatherings with meals
being the focal point for conversation. Benji told me that
Annette would come in frequently with her husband, and
sometimes her children and relatives, and on occasion reserve
a table for 12 or more for family seating. She was particularly
fond of pickled tongue Basquaise.

Benji recalled that Annette and Glen had a small ranch
north of town and raised horses. He remembered Annette
as being extremely sweet, genuine and a pleasure to be with.
There is a photo of Annette and Benji autographed by Annette
on the restaurant's Facebook page. I would estimate it to be
around 30 years old. Benji said there were other photos but
he returned them to Glen as memories of the times they
had together.

Unfortunately, one thing that both the restaurant staff and
Jim Shaw agreed on was Annette's gradual decline. She began
to have problems walking, then speaking, then eventually she
had to be carried inside. It got to the point at Benji's where
Annette couldn't come inside the restaurant and they would
pick up food to go.

Nevertheless, it was part of Annette's character that she
would want to see Benji every time she came to the restaurant, even if he had to walk outside to the car. Similarly, at
the Palace, she would acknowledge the well-wishers in the
audience, even though Glen had to wave her arm for her at the

end. Annette felt a need to be with people rather than shutting herself off — especially from those with whom she had developed friendships.

Annette's decline was pretty grim, it is true. I think I prefer to remember her through the blue haze of a black & white television as opposed to the glaring detail of High Definition. I do the same with all the Mouseketeers. Viewing a life in its entirety, Annette's illness was just one part of her life as a performer, mother, family member and friend — in all of which she excelled. Even people with a passing exposure to Annette could tell she was a wonderful person: good-natured, caring, and without pretense.

So now I wonder why I drove for three hours in 100-plus degree heat to learn what I already knew. The Mouseketeers have told us what Annette was like for years. She was the most popular Mouse for a reason. Remembering back to the '50s, my mom and I watched the show to see her.

After my road trip, I looked back at some of her Mouseketeer photos and noticed something: Aside from her striking coloration and physical attractiveness, Annette radiated niceness. The concept has almost become a pejorative modernly, but Annette made people feel that they were all right with her, whoever they were. And people wanted to know her because she was *nice*. She made them feel comfortable."

Gale Harpold
Washington State Fan

Mary Lou Fitton, a Canadian fan who took over Rita Rose's Annette Fan Club in 1989, became my friend when she asked me to work on the club with her. I live in Washington state, and we talked on the phone for hours. Both of us had the phone bills to prove it! Finally, in June 1989, Lou said she was coming to visit me, and while we were at it, she announced that we'd go visit Annette for a few days.

Oh, my! What would I wear? What would I say? I was a nervous wreck! But when Annette picked us up at our California hotel and said good morning to me, it was like we had been friends forever. I'm not sure how, but she made me feel at ease.

My fondest memories of Annette were the two times I spent with her in her home, sitting at the kitchen table or in her living room just hanging out—talking, laughing and sharing stories. She always made me feel like she was interested in what I was doing and what my life was like. We'd talk about books, our kids and carpools, and how much work it was to keep our naturally curly hair under control.

Annette had a way of making everyone feel welcome and comfortable in her home. In fact, I felt so comfortable that, when she started doing the dishes after Glen fixed us all dinner, I offered to help. What a fun memory that is—helping Annette wash dishes! While doing the dishes, she sang or hummed bits and pieces from songs. She did that often during our visit and I'm not even sure if she knew she was doing it.

Helping to run the Annette Fan Club was such an honor. My job was handling the auctions, which raised money for charity or the club treasury. Annette was always very involved with the fan club, and she was always generous with

Fan/friend Gale Harpold helps Annette with the
dishes during a 1989 visit. (Photo: Lou Fitton)

donating personal items and autographing photos. During our
visit, Lou and I spent several hours with her doing nothing but
working on club business. Several times she jumped up and
came back with personal pieces of jewelry for the auctions. I
don't think two hours went by before she offered us something
to eat. (How in the world she stayed so slim is beyond me!) Her
generosity was a wonderful part of who Annette was.

During our 1991 visit, I had the chance to see Annette
interact with Jason and Gina. It was fun watching her just "be
a mom," discussing what to pack for their lunches or asking
how their day had gone. I told Annette it seemed strange that
I didn't have lunches to pack that night for my own boys, and
that this was only the second time I had gone off and left them.
Annette smiled and told me to relax and enjoy my mini-vaca-
tion, and that I deserved it.

I feel like I knew two different "Annettes": the movie star
Annette that we all felt like we knew just from watching her on
TV and in the movies, and my friend Annette, whom I visited
and talked to on the phone. She was kind and generous, and
she loved her friends and family. She always had such a positive outlook on life, even after being diagnosed with MS.

I will always cherish my visits with the "Annette" who was
my friend.

Lou Fitton

Canadian Fan Club President

I first met Annette when Rita Rose invited me to join her and Bonnie Wendt at the rehearsals for the *Mickey Mouse Club's* 25th reunion show in 1980. I had dreamed of meeting Annette for so many years! I was completely taken aback by the discovery that hearing her voice was what made the biggest impression on me. Most people say it's how tiny she was, or how deep brown her eyes were, that they noticed first. But for me, it was that unique, unforgettable voice.

Lou Fitton is a Canadian fan who ran the Annette Collectors Club and later became a friend. (1990 photo: Bonnie Wendt)

We didn't become friends that year; I was just one of the fan club members who was lucky enough to be a friend of Rita's. But several years later, Rita was busy writing her first book, and she couldn't give the fan club as much time. It was a big job, and I was thrilled when she offered it to me. That's when my friendship with Annette came into its own.

Because I live in Canada, Annette and I spent a lot of time on the phone, exchanged numerous letters and had some great visits whenever I flew to L.A. The highlights of the visits were shared with the club members in journals but the phone calls were mostly ours alone. Sometimes the calls involved Gale Harpold, who helped me with the fan club and also was a friend of Annette's. We often talked on Thursdays when all three of our husbands were out. It consistently amazed me that Annie—as she liked us to call her—took the time to chat with us, and made each phone visit a special treat for good friends.

I always got a kick out of her sense of humor. One day she picked up the phone and heard me screaming, "I'm gonna kill the plumber!" Very seriously, she asked me what method I intended to use, "Because being a Canadian, I know you don't have a gun." Well, of course I ended up laughing and the plumber was spared.

Time has not made her passing easier for me. But it was a privilege and great fun being Annette's friend for so many years. I miss her.

Steve Stevens

Actor and Talent Agent

People who followed Annette's early career know the name Steve Stevens, who was cast as Drew Stafford, Roberta Shore's boyfriend, in the *Mickey Mouse Club's* "Annette" serial. Although he was a few years older than the other teenagers in the serial, his youthful looks made him seem younger. In 1963, Steve gave up acting to become a talent agent. He opened his own talent agency in 1976, The Stevens Group, which he still operates today with his sons.

Steve first met Annette several months before he was cast in the serial when his friend, Disney actor Sammy Ogg, took him to a party at the house of another Disney actor, Kevin "Moochie" Corcoran. "All the Mouseketeers were there, a photographer took photos which wound up at Disney, and someone said that Annette and I looked great together," Steve recalls. "So I started doing photo layouts with her, like in an ice cream parlor, and we started going out together via Disney setups. A photographer was always there. Then the part came up in the serial and Sammy's mother, who was an agent, said they were looking for someone who didn't look like a blond Disney kid. So she called the casting director and brought me in, and he immediately went to the producer who walked me straight into Walt Disney's office. I didn't have to read or audition, and Disney said I looked like a young Tony Curtis!"

During filming of the series, Steve remembers Annette being totally professional on the set and treating everyone with respect and friendship. She got along great with the director, Charles Lamont, who had believed in Annette's acting ability and later directed her in *Zorro*. "Because she was one of Disney's biggest stars and getting her first series, she handled it like a sweet teenager, just one of the gang," says Steve. "At that point, she was on the verge of being a big star. Everyone loved her."

After the "Annette" serial, Steve remained friends with Annette, Roberta and Annette's friend Shelley Fabares, who also was in the cast. Movie magazines in the early '60s were full of photos of Steve on dates with the three girls. There was no serious romance with Annette, he says, but he became one of her frequent escorts to events such as The Emmy Awards, The Academy Awards and other Hollywood events.

"People thought we were lovers, but we never were, just good friends," he recalls. "I became Annette's beau and teens around the world were jealous. We had good times together. We'd drive to Malibu and get something to eat, then hold hands and walk on the beach."

In 1958, Charles Lamont was directing Disney's *Zorro* TV series starring Guy Williams, who was Annette's big crush. Lamont thought that Steve was perfect for the role of Don Rodolfo and the young actor joined the cast.

"One day Annette came by to visit me on the set and spent almost the whole day with me on the back lot," Steve recalls. "While we were there, Guy came over and said, 'Annette, I heard you're going to do a couple of episodes.' She looked at me, then him, like a big-eyed puppy dog. She jumped up and hugged him, then pulled herself back like she was embarrassed. Then she hugged me. Here she was, this big star, and she was like a little kid who had gotten a wish come true. She couldn't control her emotions. It was really special."

The role was indeed a 16th birthday gift from Walt Disney himself, who was well aware of Annette's crush on Guy Williams.

One of Steve's most special memories of Annette occurred when, at 19, he joined the Marines. On a Friday night, he called Annette to tell her he was leaving for boot camp on Monday.

"She told me to come over to her house, and when I got there she said she wanted to take me somewhere. She drove us to St. Charles Catholic Church in Hollywood. When we got there she grabbed my hand and we went into the church, and walked all the way to altar. She held my hand and said, 'Let's pray. I just want you to be safe.' Then she hugged me and we both teared up a little. I couldn't believe it, it was so special. Afterwards we didn't say much, just got into the car and went back to her house. She said she would write to me and pray for me. Of all the time I spent with her, this was my special moment."

While Steve was in boot camp, Annette wrote to him frequently. When one of his drill instructors saw the mail from Disney, he asked Steve who it was from. "When I said it was Annette, he said, 'You mean the Mouseketeer? Can you get me an autographed picture for my daughter?' So I bartered photos for not having to peel potatoes," Steve laughs.

Getting signed photos of Annette for other people became a cottage industry for Steve. As a teen actor, he played several roles as a juvenile delinquent, which came to the

Actor-turned-agent Steve Stevens was a close friend of
Annette's and escorted her to many Hollywood events.
This was taken at the Golden Globes in March 1960.

attention of a gangster named Mickey Cohen. They became friends and, unfortunately, Cohen had a negative influence on Steve's career. It was during this time that Steve used autographed pictures of Annette to pay off favors among Cohen's gang members.

"When people found out I knew Annette they always asked me to get her autograph for them," he recalls. "The Mafia guys wanted pictures of Annette for themselves and relatives—they just loved her. She was my pocket of gold!" (He and longtime friend Craig Lockwood wrote the 2006 book *King of the Sunset Strip*, about Steve's relationship with Mickey Cohen.)

The last time Steve saw Annette was in 1986 when she did a guest appearance on *Growing Pains*. Cast member Andrew Koenig, son of *Star Trek* actor Walter Koenig, called

Steve Stevens and Annette from the *Mickey Mouse Club's* "Annette" serial in 1958. (Photo © The Walt Disney Company)

Steve to let him know Annette was on the show. Koenig knew Steve had worked with her in the past.

"Annette said she'd love to see me, so she left me a pass and I went on the set at Warner Bros.," says Steve. "Annette was sitting there in a chair with the cast and crew lined up, bringing stuff for her to sign and sharing their memorabilia with each other. You'd have thought the President had shown up at Warner Bros.! So I get in line and hand her a photo of the two of us, and she did a double-take! She jumped up and gave me a big hug and kiss."

After the signing, Annette and Steve went to the commissary to grab some lunch. This was a year before she was diagnosed with MS and some of her symptoms were beginning to show.

"We were walking along and she grabs my arm, and I asked her what was the matter? She said she had a little cold. We sat down on the steps of a trailer for a bit, then got up and walked a little slower, talking about old times. I said 'Let's get a cart,' and she said OK, so we took a cart the rest of the way. After lunch, I took her to makeup, gave her a kiss and hug. Then I left."

When Annette's MS was made public in 1992, it upset her longtime friend tremendously. But he keeps his good memories close, along with the confidences she shared with him.

"I kept her secrets," he reveals. "It's hard to explain when someone is so real and goodhearted.

"I liked her parents very much. Her dad had his little mechanic shop, a good old blue-collar Italian guy who didn't seem to be in awe over her fame. People would come into his shop and see pictures of Annette on the wall and he'd never tell anyone that it was his daughter. Now Virginia, she wound up being one of those show business parents. I think Virginia would have liked to put a tattoo on her forehead saying that Annette was her daughter!"

Connie Francis
Singer

The TV show *American Bandstand* was a phenomenal success with teenagers across the country, and two of its most popular guests were Annette and Connie Francis, both of whom toured with Dick Clark's Caravan of Stars in the late 1950s and early '60s. Connie was an international singing sensation who recorded in several languages. On the home front, her hits included "Who's Sorry Now?", "Stupid Cupid," "My Happiness," "Lipstick on Your Collar" and "Among My Souvenirs." She had roles in a few early '60s movies, including *Follow the Boys* and *Where the Boys Are,* and performed in nightclubs and other venues as well. While she was a few years older than the Teen Idols of the day, she still fit in with the rock 'n' roll music of her peers.

Although they weren't close friends, Annette and Connie had the Italian connection. They were both from the East, and in addition had a shared Catholic heritage. Their career paths often intersected, and whenever they ran into each other their friendship would be rekindled. Annette treasured a Lucite piece with an inspirational saying on it, given to her by Connie early in their careers. She kept it in her living room where visitors would easily see it.

"I would often make up a saying to put on Lucite and send it to people that I liked," Connie recalls. "I remember sending one to Annette, although I don't recall what it said. She was one of sweetest people I ever met, just an angel."

They also bonded over their mutual admiration for singer Bobby Darin, who for a time was Connie's love interest.

"Annette commented to me that Bobby was a great talent who never got the recognition he deserved," says Connie. "He

WAS the best entertainer ever. No one could compete with Bobby because he was so versatile—a great actor, musician and songwriter. I was glad that Annette saw that, too."

At the height of their popularity in the 1960s, Connie constantly was amused by fans who would see her and believe she was Annette.

"That happened a lot. We were both little Italian girls and looked alike. I wasn't as pretty as Annette, but people would often mistake me for her. If they asked me for an autograph, I told them, 'Sorry, I'm not Annette!'"

Connie remembers special times spent with Annette and Paul Anka, who were having a teen romance in 1959. "Once, we were at Frankie Avalon's house for dinner and someone took a cute picture of Annette sitting in Paul's lap. She was deeply in love with Paul, but he wasn't ready to get married."

The singer was greatly saddened when she learned that Annette had MS. "I spoke to her by phone when she was still able to speak. It was a tragedy how her life ended. So sad," she says.

Connie wrote her first autobiography, *Who's Sorry Now?*, in 1984. Her second, *Among My Souvenirs: The Real Story, Vol. 1*, was published in 2017.

Kathy Maraldo

"Twin" Friend

In 1985, Annette began a love affair with New Orleans. It was the first of several years in which she went to the Big Easy to be either Grand Marshal or a guest of the Italian-American St. Joseph's Day Parade, which honors the patron saint of Sicily. It's organized by the Italian-American Marching Club, an all-male society of which Tony Russo, a criminal court judge, is a founding member. For this initial visit, on the day Annette was to arrive, Tony asked his sister, Kathy Maraldo, to accompany the 25 male officers to the airport. Kathy was more than happy to do that: Not only was she a fan of Annette's, she also strongly resembled her. They hit it off immediately, and that day was the start of a special friendship. Here is Kathy's story:

The IAMC is an organization consisting of men only and Annette was traveling with her father. Although security and bodyguards are always present, the directors felt that Annette could be made more comfortable by being accompanied to restrooms, hotel rooms and restaurants with another female. So my brother Tony asked me to come to the airport and greet her. How could I refuse?

Annette got off the plane wearing a beautiful white sweater with chevrons of red and green feathers, and my brother handed her a bouquet of red roses. She was absolutely stunning. Then she said, "You look like me!" I said, "Maybe you look like me?" She said, "I think that I am older." So I said, "You win!"

Her dad was called "Mr. Joe" and he was dearly loved by all. He was a celebrity in his own right in New Orleans. He always said that New Orleans reminded him of being in the Italian communities of his former upstate New York home.

Every year, St. Joseph's Day is a tremendous celebration because of the large Sicilian population in New Orleans. In the 15th century, during a terrible famine in Sicily, these Italians prayed to St. Joseph for help to feed their families. The rains came, crops began to grow and the families survived. To honor St. Joseph, each year many Italian families prepare large altars laden with food in their homes and open their doors to feed everyone. The Saint Joseph parade, with its chariots, floats, princesses, queen and 1500 marchers, is the last parade that is allowed to go through the French Quarter at night. It's a fun celebration and Annette loved it.

New Orleans is a unique city...celebrities can usually walk through the French Quarter and no one bothers them because they're a familiar sight. Some are very demanding and you have to entertain them, but Annette was totally different. On her first night here, she told Tony she had to pay him for a phone call she made to check on her kids because "it wasn't in the contract." Tony laughed and said it was absolutely fine and to call home any time.

One afternoon, as we were relaxing between events in her hotel room, I told Annette that she made my teenage years fabulous. She asked how, and I said that I went to a parochial grammar school in a predominately Irish-American neighborhood. Most of the little girls were blue-eyed blondes; I stood out with my dark curly hair and big brown eyes. I always wanted to look like everybody else. "All of a sudden," I told her, "the *Mickey Mouse Club* started and there you were. Every boy in America was in love with you! It turned my life around and it was just great." She laughed and said, "I never thought of it that way but I felt the same way because all of the other Disney Mouseketeers had freckles and blue eyes. I was the only ethnic one."

Our relationship was so easy and comfortable. Although Annette was a movie star and lived in Hollywood, she and I were daughters of second-generation Italian immigrants and we were raised with the values instilled in us by our parents and large extended families. We both married Italian men and had teenage children the same ages.

Wherever we were, there was no getting around the comparison of our appearance. Once we went into a French Quarter restaurant, and when I walked in the maitre d'

Kathy Maraldo met Annette in 1985 during the St. Joseph Day festivities in New Orleans. The lookalikes became close friends and visited each other often. (1991 photo: Nick Strange)

extended his hand and said, "It's a pleasure to have you at Antoine's." Then Annette walked in and he did a double take! We got a good laugh out of that. Another time, Fabian was here to promote a movie and he, too, told me that I looked like Annette. Frankie Avalon even asked Annette why she had hidden her sister all these years! This reaction was constant and made each of us uncomfortable.

Annette and I stayed together all weekend and we had many great conversations before their flight left on Sunday. She said to me, "Gee, I wish you lived closer." Celebrities don't say that!

After she got home, we wrote to each other regularly. As luck would have it, my brother had a heart attack and her son Jacky had been in a motorcycle accident, so we began to call one another at least twice a week. I knew that she was getting serious with Glen, and one afternoon she called and said, "Guess what?" I said, "You are going to marry Glen." I flew to California and lent a hand with shopping for her wedding dress, invitations and reception plans.

That was the beginning of my California visits. While she was in New Orleans, Annette had discovered the Muffaletta, an Italian sandwich that came on a big piece of olive oil-soaked round bread with salami, prosciutto ham and several cheeses. She would have had it for breakfast, lunch and dinner if she

could! When I went to California I'd bring her an ice chest full
of those sandwiches. No one could touch them. She also became
fond of white chocolate bread pudding, so I brought her that, too.

Annette loved New Orleans in part because she knew,
beyond a doubt, that she was completely safe and very pro-
tected there. In all of the years and the many times that
she visited the city, there was never an article written by
anyone, an unflattering picture given to anyone or any story
or excursion reported by anyone to any news source. She was
totally free and happy here, though some fans couldn't resist
approaching her, and felt a most wonderful and welcomed
sense of normality. But Annette never came to New Orleans
between April and October when the humidity was so high
that it would frizz her hair. She'd say, "If you can look good
in New Orleans in the summer, you can look good anywhere!"

Annette was very bright and clever and had quite a sense of
humor. She could put in a good zinger! My children called her
Miss Annette—she loved to come to the South and be called
"Miss Annette"! We talked about our fears, hopes and dreams
for our kids and so many other things. She knew she could
always be herself with me and say what she wanted. She could
let her hair down because she knew I wanted nothing from her,
that we were established and secure in our own worlds. It was
a wonderful relationship.

Because we looked so much alike, Annette was very sen-
sitive about how we were treated in public. This was often
most difficult. Once we were at the St. Louis Cathedral in New
Orleans and a woman ran up to her for an autograph. The
woman wanted to take a picture, so as always, I took a step
back. The woman said, "Oh, get your daughter in the picture
too!" Annette looked at me, immediately saw the distress on
my face, smiled sweetly, reached out her hand, pulled me in the
picture and said, "It's OK." Later, she asked me if I had seen the
movie *Beaches*. I answered that I had not. "Go see the movie, it
explains everything that I want you to know," she said.

Well, the next day Claude and I went to see the movie. I
cried all the way through it, understanding the meaning of her
request. Later that week, Annette sent me a beautiful music
box with a unicorn inside of a big heart that played "Wind

Beneath My Wings."

Another gift story: I had a makeup bag that I loved but was beyond its prime, and she looked at it and said, "Oh, dear, we have to do better than that!" The next week I got the most phenomenally beautiful silver satin makeup bag trimmed in burgundy with my name embossed on it. I have never used it for makeup but for my favorite accessories.

Annette took great care in selecting meaningful and beautiful gifts for special occasions, or no occasion. She also sent us a porcelain cake plate with roses and "Kathy and Claude" painted on it and a beautiful emerald green enamel picture frame with our names and year engraved. When my first grandchildren were born, she sent two delightful teddy bears from her QVC collection. She loved large crystal decanters, and though the years I sent her several Waterford and Baccarat decanters and cordial glasses. To the best of my knowledge, none of these survived the 2011 fire that destroyed her house.

Eating out with her was always interesting. I sat with her many times in restaurants when middle-aged men came up to the table with the stupidest little-boy grins, trying to speak and grin at the same time. They would always start off saying, "You were my first girlfriend!" And she always answered them as if it was the first time she had heard that sentence. She acted surprised, and always made each one feel that she was flattered and that he was special. Once we were in a swanky restaurant and a man couldn't contain himself. He was a big oil executive and began to panic that we were going to soon be leaving. He followed Claude into the restroom like a kid, holding on to him and begging him to introduce him to Annette. When Claude brought him over to the table, he stammered, tried to composed himself, and blurted out, "You were my first girlfriend!" He left the restaurant with the biggest smile. Annette was always gracious and kind to everyone.

During one visit, the mayor of New Orleans found out Annette was coming and asked me to bring her to city hall. I said I wouldn't because she was coming as a friend to visit and I would not want her to feel exploited in any way. I did invite him to a private tea at the Windsor Court Hotel that I was hosting for Annette with my family. He showed up with a proclamation for Annette and gave her a key to the city! I now have the key; Dave Mason of Saturday's Toys sent it to me. (Saturday's Toys auctions Annette's personal items to raise money for The Annette Funicello Fund for Neurological Diseases.)

Around 1988, Claude and I traveled with Annette to Cincinnati where she was doing an infomercial for weight control cookies. While we were there she said she had to speak to me. We went on the shoot, went to dinner, and she forgot her glasses in the restaurant. Claude and Glen went back to the restaurant to get them. When we were alone I asked her what she wanted to tell me. She said, "It's nothing." I did not want to pry and simply allowed the subject to drop.

The next day when we kissed goodbye at the airport, she again said she had something to tell me but just couldn't. When I returned home, the phone was ringing. It was Annette. She told me that she just could not tell me in person: It was just too painful and she did not want to see my face at that moment. Then she told me of the MS diagnosis. I looked at Claude, and in a second, I knew that he knew. Glen had told him when they walked back to the restaurant to retrieve Annette's glasses. It was Annette's wish that she tell me.

After the initial shock and days of disbelief,

Kathy Maraldo, Gina and Annette at the Funicellos' 50th wedding anniversary party. (1991 photo: Nick Strange)

Annette and I discussed the prognosis and how to handle it. No one, with the exception of Glen, her mother and her kids, knew of this devastating diagnosis. Then Annette called one afternoon to tell me that Frankie had extended the prospect of going on the road for a concert tour. Her doctors didn't want her to do it because it would be stressful. I said, "Do you want to do this?" She said yes, and I told her that I would meet her as many times as I could. She was just beginning to have difficulty walking and with balance. Her eyesight was also rapidly deteriorating.

After her first rehearsal, she called me and said, "It was awful, I can't sing anymore." I laughed and said, "You never could sing!" Then she laughed and said, "What did you say?" Tickets were $17 and the show was 90 minutes. So I told her, "In that hour-and-a-half you can take a person back to a time in their life when they were young, beautiful, happy and with a life full of hope and expectations, and you can do that for $17. This is no small gift! If they wanted to see a singer, they would go hear Barbra Streisand. All people want to see is you with Frankie. Can you possibility manage *Tall Paul* and *Pineapple Princess*?" She laughed and said, "I knew there was a reason I called. There must be an insult in there but I can't find it." That's the kind of honest and fun relationship we had.

As her MS progressed, I used to meet her at MD Anderson Hospital in Houston when she was doing experimental treatments. The doctors would draw her blood, then spin the blood, attempt to extract the good cells and then inject the healthy cells back into her system with the hope of reinforcing her immune system. We would go to lunch, rest, travel around the hospital and shop in between doctor's visits. While my presence there did not mitigate the pain, we were able to spend quiet and important time alone having meaningful, personal discussions. She always told me that my coming to Houston made the treatments bearable because she always looked forward to seeing me and having me with her.

I started spending more time in California. We saw the Golden Boys of Bandstand at the Hollywood Bowl with Frankie, Fabian and Bobby Rydell. Annette was there as a surprise guest, then we went to an after-party. In 1991, Claude and I flew to

Palm Springs for her parents' 50th anniversary celebration. It was a beautiful affair and a wonderful party. Annette had a beautiful beaded dress but was now wearing very low heels and not the stilettos that she loved and had always worn.

By the time Gina got married in 1994, Annette was in a wheelchair. At Gina's wedding Annette and Glen were seated at a table by the dance floor. Claude and I sat at the next table, Minnie and Mickey Mouse came in, and the night was magical. Frankie Avalon, Gina's godfather, sang *Bobby Sox to Stockings* to the bride.

The next morning, there was a lovely brunch given by the groom's parents. I was seated on one side of Annette and Glen was on the other side of her. When the food came, Glen picked up the fork to feed Annette, and my whole body started to tremble. That's when "it" became unbearably real. In the six months since I had last seen her, the changes were rapid and devastating. As long as we could go to lunch, talk and laugh, the realism of her illness was put aside for the moment. Until this time, Annette had maintained the use of her hands, and even after she was confined to a wheelchair we were able to have somewhat normal excursions.

In the years after the wedding, I would fly to California for a visit and Annette would want to go out. I was constantly amazed by her courage. I learned how to feed her. One of her favorite places was an Italian restaurant that had a booth recessed behind a door. They would seat us there and I would feed her, and tease her about how it's a good thing Italians feed each other. Annette took everything with such dignity and courage. Once again, we had successfully climbed another hill.

During our talks, she said something very profound to me. I wanted her opinion as to whether or not I should do something that I wanted to do. I will never forget her words to me. She wanted me to do it, and I can still hear her voice as she said:

"The last day in your life is not the day you die, it's the day you are diagnosed. When you leave the hospital after the diagnosis, from that moment on you never laugh as freely or smile as freely. Your illness is on your mind constantly, and from that moment on, life as you knew it to be is over. Then it becomes a series of doctors' offices and treatment plans. You view everything in the context of the rapidity of your illness and how rapidly it will progress. You view every day in the prism of your death."

The last day I saw her was in 1998. We had watched *Babes in Toyland* the night before, and the next morning I went into her room and sat on her bed. Her voice was very shaky and measured, and she asked me, "Kath, do you think I'll dance in heaven?" Yes, I said. I told her that she would dance every day in heaven for eternity and that "Walt will take care of you." She asked me if I promised. I said yes, and asked her if I had ever broken a promise to her. She said very definitively, "NO!" Then I smiled and said, "You still won't sing worth a damn." I told her that she would need a backup choir of angels and 50 harps. She laughed and laughed.

Her last words to me were "I love you," and I answered, "I love you too." I cried from California to New Orleans because I knew it was the last time I'd see my precious friend. After that, the nurses would call and place the phone by her ear so that I could speak to her.

Annette was used to being the go-to person in her family. She was the caretaker. She tried to meet each increment of her limitations with dignity, and on a plane I could not hope to achieve. My time with her was precious and thank God I had the sense to know it then. I consider her one of the best friends in my life.

As my brother Tony once said in a toast to her, "You were every boy's first love and every girl's best friend. You are America's Sweetheart. We have always loved you and you have given your love back to America and to the world."

I was so very fortunate that, in the most unexpected turn of fate, my life was not only to touch but to bind with this truly beautiful child of God. She was the best and most loving friend anyone could have the privilege to enjoy, sharing joys, sorrows, dreams, hopes and fears. She was never judgmental and always caring and supportive. Although I was frightened and devastated upon learning of her illness, she accepted her diagnosis with unbelievable fortitude. As the disease progressed and her abilities failed, she again accepted these debilitating changes without complaint.

Annette was an inspiration and successfully achieved a plateau of grace that I can only aspire to work toward, but know that I can never attain.

Donna Gaffin

New York Fan

This story is from a 1977 Annette Fan Club journal.

The biggest thrills of my life came in 1964 and 1966 when I got to meet Annette in person. I'd been a fan since the age of 9, watching the *Mickey Mouse Club*.

The show ended, but Annette's career continued, and my idolization of her continued with it. On June 18, 1960, when I was 12 years old, I got my first chance to see her in person at Radio City Music Hall in New York. But being as young as I was, I never thought to try to meet her. I didn't see her in person again until age 14, when she was making personal appearances for Walt Disney Studios at movie theaters in New York. I was thrilled to attend two of them and was even able to take some pictures!

Annette came back the next year and I tried to think of every possible way to meet my idol. My girlfriend Pat and I went to the local Disney offices, thinking maybe Annette had appointments there, but to our disappointment, she didn't. Little did I know that, three months later, I would finally get to meet her.

The World's Fair that year was held in New York, and on July 4, 1964, Annette was there with Frankie Avalon, Buddy Hackett and Harvey Lembeck. The beach movies were popular then and Annette put her handprints in cement outside of the Hollywood Pavilion. Pat and I were so excited to watch the ceremony—and afterwards, to actually speak with her! We asked her to sign a few pictures that we had taken at the movie theaters. I asked her if she was going to do any more shows in the area, and she said she was going to be at the Better Living Exhibition. Naturally, Pat and I went to that, and got more autographs!

The theater in the pavilion for the Better Living Exhibition was showing the premiere of *Bikini Beach* for the celebrities and press, or by special invitation. We were floored when Disney's public relations gal, Arlene Ludwig, asked if we'd like to come in and see the movie. Of course, we immediately accepted the invitation! Afterwards, we got to talk to Annette again. We told her how good she was, and she very graciously thanked us. Jack Gilardi was there too—at that time he and Annette had just gotten engaged. In answer to my question, she said she didn't know yet when the wedding would be. When I asked if she was going to give up her career, she smiled and said, "Yes, after a while."

We reluctantly said our goodbyes and rushed to the store to get our film developed. It was then that we realized, to our dismay, that we never had our own pictures taken with Annette! We vowed if we ever got another chance to meet her, we would make sure to get a picture with her.

Two years later, we got our second chance. Annette was appearing on *The Ed Sullivan Show*, and I didn't find out until a few days before the show that tickets were always gone months in advance. Pat and I went to the theater anyway, and arrived in time for rehearsals. To our great joy, there were empty seats, so we got in! As it turned out, there were even empty seats for the regular show! Arlene was sitting behind us and we showed her the photos of Annette at the World's Fair. After the show, we hung around in the lobby until Annette and Jack came down the elevator. When we showed our photos to Annette, she exclaimed, "Oh, these must be the ones Arlene was talking about!" I took a picture of her and Jack cheek-to-cheek, then Annie very sweetly posed with us before leaving.

I hope that, some day, I'll meet her again during one of my trips to California. But even if I don't, I know I've been luckier than most fans in that I met her twice, and I'll never forget how nice she was to two New York fans.

(Donna has since passed away, but she did meet Annette again in California in the 1980s.)

Thomas Pickles
California Fan

I turned 40 on Dec. 26, 1988. It's a lousy day for a birthday and usually passes by without much ado amid the holiday hangovers—which is fine with me. At the time, I was working at an ad agency in Los Angeles. Unbeknownst to me, my friends there decided to cook up a surprise party for me. Because everyone at the agency was scattered for the holidays, my actual birthday came and went as usual—which made their "surprise" shenanigans all the more effective when we all went back to work in early January.

My co-workers knew I had been an Annette fan since I was a teenager; I had her *Annette's Beach Party* album framed on my office wall as kitschy décor. So, for my 40th birthday, they tried to arrange—on a "top secret" basis—for Annette to show up. Unfortunately, she said she was unable to come, but had offered to call me instead.

On the day of the ambush, I was called into the main conference room for an impromptu meeting, which was nothing unusual. When I walked into the room, I was greeted by "Surprise!" Half of the agency was there...along with my clients. A colleague handed me the phone and said, "Someone wants to speak with you." Not knowing what to expect, I took the phone and said "Hello?" When I heard "Hello, Tom," I knew instantly who it was. I replied, "Oh...it's *you!*" It was humiliating, but she chuckled. Making matters worse, the phone call had been piped into the agency PA system, so my fumbling dialogue was being broadcast to everyone.

It was a short conversation. I don't even remember what was said. But afterwards I got her address and sent her a rare album by her *Mickey Mouse Club* friend, Jimmie Dodd, and thanked her for being a good sport. I got a handwritten letter from her a few days later.

This happened not too long after she had discovered that she had MS. I suspect she didn't attend my party because she was still somewhat off balance (both physically and emotionally) and didn't really want to be the object of such embarrassing scrutiny, even with a relatively private gathering.

In any case, she was very kind to play along with the phone call (especially given what was going on in her life at the time) and she left me with a treasured memory and a personal letter. The lady was pure class.

Virginia Funicello
Mother

Annette's mom, Virginia, was an extraordinary woman. When Annette was a Mouseketeer, Virginia—known to friends and family as Virgie—was required by state law to be at the studio with her all day. She had to balance that duty with taking care of Annette's two younger brothers, Joey and Mike, as well as running her household in Studio City. Her life as a Mouseke-mom was challenging, a fact she acknowledged in this interview in one of the Annette Fan Club publications:

"When Annette became a Mouseketeer," Virginia related, "our life completely changed. First of all, they told me there was a California law that the parent had to be with the child ALL DAY LONG. Even when she was in school."

The restriction made things awkward, since the youngest Funicello was still a toddler. "Michael was 2 years old and I had no one to watch him. I was going to hire one of my friends to sit with Annette, but she wouldn't let anyone sit with her but me. She was only 12 and so shy. I had a girlfriend, Michael's godmother, and she said she would take care of him if we dropped him off, because she lived near Disney Studios. He would cry all day long until I picked him up at 6. I tried putting him in a nursery school near the studio. He was there one day because he cried and cried."

Virginia's solution was made out of desperation.

"Then I started sneaking home. The guard at the front gate knew my situation. I'd pick up Michael, make a big dinner, wash clothes, then rush back. The guard would tell people I was in the mail room or the public relations office. We cheated. We had to." Virginia laughed as she confessed, "I thought the studio teacher never knew about it until the 25th anniversary of the show and I told her. And she said, 'I knew where you went and what time you came back.' She let me get away with it!"

The Disney show ran for three seasons and definitely impacted the Funicellos' lives.

"I think the *Mickey Mouse Club* affected Joey more than it affected Michael," said Virginia, recalling that "Michael hated the idea of me leaving him every day, but Joey was older. The kids would laugh about (the *Mickey Mouse*

Virginia and Joe with baby Annette in Utica, N.Y., where she was born.
(Photo: Nick Strange Collection)

Club) and it was tough on Joey. Annette became very popular and the kids all wanted to come to the house. Not for him, but to see Annette. He went through quite a bad period with that. When he graduated from high school we wanted to give him a nice, big surprise party, but he found out about it. He said there'd be about 100 kids coming in, so he just didn't want it."

Annette's popularity continued to grow. "When Joey was in high school the boys were all in love with Annette. She went on one of those DJ shows one night that was popular with all the kids. She said some weird thing like, 'Oh, now that my brother's interested in girls he's in the shower all the time.' Joey was mortified...she meant that he was always cleaning up! The kids in school ribbed him about that."

Michael took things in stride. Virginia chuckled at the remembrance of one of his pranks.

"When Michael was older and Annette was really popular, the paperboy wanted to get a look at her. Michael said, 'Give

me a dollar and I'll let you see her!' So the kid gave him half of
a dollar bill. Annette was getting up and had her nightgown
on, and when she opened the refrigerator Michael opened the
door to let the paperboy see her. He gave Michael the other
half of the dollar. It didn't bother him at all that his sister was
a celebrity. He pulled things like that."

Virginia did a lot of traveling with Annette when she was
still a minor, from the Mouseketeer days to personal appearances for movies and TV. In later years, Virginia loved to be
around when fans came to visit Annette at her own home.
She always wanted to feed them, and she always had plenty of
tales to share. Storytelling was her calling. She was funny and
animated and cheerful, and those of us lucky enough to meet
her all came to love her as much as we loved Annette.

Virginia passed away in 2007 at age 86. Annette's dad, Joe,
died in 2009 at 93.

Annette with aunts Josephine Monaco, Carmella Barletto,
mom Virginia and aunt Mickie Gadicola, all Virginia's sisters.
1990 photo in Utica. (Photo: Nick Strange Collection)

Miscellaneous Quotes

Tommy Sands, singer/actor: I did *Babes in Toyland* with Annette and she was great to work with. The opening scene where we're dancing, we had to rehearse six or seven times because I'm such a bad dancer! It took me months to learn it! Annette was beautiful—she was America's Sweetheart.

Excerpts of a 1992 letter to Annette from **Mouseketeer Bobby Burgess** that appeared in his autobiography, *Ears and Bubbles: Dancing My Way from the Mickey Mouse Club to The Lawrence Welk Show* (Theme Park Press):

> Dear Annette,
>
> I guess you could call me part of your Mouse-ka-support system along with Tommy, Sharon, Lonnie, Sherry and, of course, Lorraine. We're all there for you....I realize now why you didn't go skating at my 50th birthday party. But I was proud you came and proud to introduce you to everyone.
>
> Did you know I didn't get a traffic ticket recently because of you? Yeah, as I was speeding down Nichols Canyon, a radar cop pulled me over. He recognized me as a Mouseketeer, then said, 'I won't give you a ticket if you'll tell me about Annette!' Of course, I had to tell him that you were the same as when I first met you thirty-five years ago, down-to-earth, and just the same friendly person you always were.
>
> Well, Consentrina, 'hope to see you real soon.' I'll be thinking of you.
>
> Love, your dancin' Mouseka pal, Bobby B.

Don Grady, Mouseketeer: Who doesn't love Annette? She gave me my first kiss...on the forehead! But hey, she will always be my favorite girl.

Tommy Cole, Mouseketeer: I was very close with Annie. We spent a lot of years together and I loved her dearly. When my wife had back surgery and was in a lot of pain, Annie called Aileen to help her get through it. She gave Aileen a lot of support and love and was always very concerned about other people.

Cubby O'Brien, Mouseketeer: Since Annette was older than I was during our years together on the *Mickey Mouse Club*, I don't have any details to share other than she was a wonderful, talented person who was loved by all.

Diane Disney Miller, Walt Disney's daughter: Everyone who knew Annette loved and respected her. She was one of the loveliest people I've ever known, and was always so kind to everyone. She was also the consummate professional and had such great loyalty to my father. She will always be very special to me.

Lori Loughlin, costar in 1987's *Back to the Beach*: Annette Funicello was really a wonderful person. I enjoyed working with her immensely and found her to be kind and down-to-earth. She faced her illness with courage and never wanted anyone to have pity on her.

Ernie Garcia, fan: Annette Funicello was not only beautiful and talented, she was never a threat to other girls. Both guys and girls appreciated who she was and felt that she deserved the adulation that she received. Annette had something special that kids identified with. Teenagers have insecurities and so did she. Annette was shy, non-threatening and always positive. Perhaps that was the magic ingredient that made her beautiful in so many ways.

Unknown fan: Annette Funicello was always very poised, stylish and feminine. She knew exactly how to stand and how to pose even as a very young girl. It's obvious why she stood out from the rest of the Mouseketeers. She wasn't competing, either. It just came very natural and sweet-like. She never quite understood what the attention to her was all about because she was so shy and sometimes even felt inferior to the other kids on the show. Her dark features obviously made her stand out, and ethnic audience viewers could relate to her. Annette was a role model for many kids and they learned that you didn't really have to be blonde or blue-eyed to be very, very popular!

From the press book for *The Golden Horseshoe Review*: In 1962, Annette was cast in the Disney film *The Golden Horseshoe Review* only a day before shooting was scheduled to begin. Actor Henry Calvin was originally slated to appear in the project but had just suffered a slight heart attack, necessitating that the project be recast. The film's producer, **Ron Miller**, reached out to Annette to see if she might be available on such last-minute notice. Without asking anything about the part, she simply said "yes" and showed up the next day for her wardrobe fitting, ready to do whatever she could to help "Mr. Disney." She learned the songs "Buffalo Round-up," "Hang a Lantern in Your Window" and "Mr. Piano Man" in just one day. Ron never forgot Annette's support and her kindness, particularly on what is regarded as his first official film as a director at the Walt Disney Studio.

Bette Midler, singer, in a tweet after Annette died: WE ALL LOVED YOU!

Annette Memorial Speech

June 24, 2013
Disney Studio Theatre
Burbank, Calif.

Two months after Annette passed away, her children, Gina, Jacky and Jason, invited Bonnie Wendt and me to a special celebration of her life at Disney Studios. That same day, Stage 1, the home of the Mickey Mouse Club, was dedicated as the Annette Funicello Stage by Walt Disney Company Chairman and CEO Bob Iger. In the audience were friends, family, colleagues and Mouseketeers. Bonnie and I offered this tribute to Annette:

In 1956, a 9-year-old girl named Suzanne stood in line at Disneyland to get autographs from Annette, Tim Considine and David Stollery from the *Mickey Mouse Club's* "Spin and Marty" series. It was set up for the kids in line to get an autographed paper from Spin, then take it to Annette and then Marty for their signatures. Somehow, Spin didn't notice her, but Annette saw this sad little girl and asked if she wanted her to sign her paper. "Spin didn't give me one," Suzanne sobbed. Annette immediately took Spin to task, got the paper and got all the signatures for her. It's one of her great childhood memories and, of course, it made Annette her hero!

Annette's compassion for others is among many reasons that she was loved by her fans. I also was 9 when Annette and the Mouseketeers came into my life, and at 15 I started one of Annette's fan clubs that ran for 28 years. This is Bonnie Wendt, who also ran a fan club, and that's how we became long-distance friends back in high school.

We started out as fans of Annette's, but had no idea that we would eventually become her friend. We met her for the first time when we were just teenagers and she invited us to her wedding to Jack Gilardi. Through the years, we visited her home several times where she was a gracious hostess. Even her parents, Virginia and Joe, would welcome fans into their home. Eventually, the lines blurred between fan and friend.

Most people of my generation became fans because of the *Mickey Mouse Club*. We loved all the Mouseketeers, and it's hard to say exactly why we were drawn to Annette. She had a shy, sweet smile and a special charismatic light. With over 6,000 fan letters a day, she was charming an entire nation. And she never really understood what the fuss was all about, which made her more endearing.

After the show went off the air, we followed Annette through her singing career, her Disney films and the beach movies with Frankie Avalon. Some people became fans as she made a seamless transition from child star to adult star. Our fan clubs grew along with her popularity.

Before the Internet, fan club correspondence was done by mail. And now, many of the original fans stay in touch through an online Yahoo group I started in 2004. When I found out I would be speaking at this memorial, I asked the group's members to provide words or phrases that described Annette. Here are some of them: Humble, beautiful, down-to-earth, amazing, sweet, beloved, a role model, full of grace, sense of humor and an example of how to treat others. One thing that's special about meeting her fans is finding out that most of them share the same positive traits that Annette had. If you say you're an Annette fan, we already know a lot about you.

Annette always said that she would never take a TV or movie role that would embarrass her family or fans. And you know what? She never disappointed us. We could count on her to entertain us and live a normal life devoid of gossip and scandal. And when her career slowed down while she was raising her kids, we were still interested in what was going on in her life.

Even with her busy life, Annette always made time for her fans. She would send them handwritten letters, sometimes call them on the phone, and send gifts. Her thoughtfulness was amazing and enduring.

If you Google her name and read all the tributes, you will find that not one person had anything bad to say about Annette. Not one. That truly sums up her character.

Bonnie and I have been friends for a long time, and we also have longtime friendships with other fans. We still call, write and visit. And while Annette gave us a lot of pleasure as a singer, dancer and actress, the best gift she ever gave us was each other.

When she sang "Through the years we'll all be friends," she wasn't kidding. I think I can speak for all of her fans around the world when I say thank you from the tips of our Mickey Mouse Ears to the bottom of our hearts.

We'd also like to thank Disney Studios for letting us visit over the years, especially during filming of *The Mouseketeer Reunion* 25th anniversary in 1980. And a special thanks to Disney publicist Arlene Ludwig, who helped us so much with material for our fan clubs.

Annette's children, Jacky (left), Gina and Jason, at Gina's wedding rehearsal in 1994. Jacky became a film producer, Gina does entertainment marketing, and Jason is a professional drummer. (Photo: Nick Strange)

Family and friends gathered for Gina's wedding in 1994. Back (from left) Glen Holt and Nick Strange; front (from left) Annette, Sharon Baird, Joe Funicello, Virginia Funicello and Shelley Fabares. (Photo: Nick Strange Collection)

Annette clowns around with her cousin, Frankie Barletto, circa 1952. (Photo: Nick Strange Collection)

Annette poses in her Mouseketeer outfit at Disney Studios in 1955. She was always baffled by her popularity on the *Mickey Mouse Club*. (Photo: Nick Strange Collection)

Annette took dance and drumming lessons at a young age. Her mom, Virginia, made most of her outfits. (Photo: Nick Strange Collection)

Even as a youngster Annette had great fashion sense as she shows off this cute dress. (Photo: Nick Strange Collection)

Young Annette in an old family photo, circa 1950. (Photo: Nick Strange Collection)

Annette's brothers Joe (left) and Mike with their parents on their 50th wedding anniversary celebration in 1991. (Photo: Nick Strange)

A sweet moment between Annette and her first husband, Jack Gilardi, in 1972. (Photo: Rita Rose)

This was Annette's favorite photo of her with second husband Glen Holt, 1991. (Photo: Nick Strange)

Rita's friend Kathy Russell came along on a 1985 visit to Annette's home. (Photo: Rita Rose)

World's Tallest Woman
Sandy Allen, who was
7-foot-7, gave 5-foot-3
Annette someone
to look up to. (1978
photo: Rita Rose)

Ohio fan club member Mary Lou Wallace was thrilled to
meet Annette for the first time after Annette and Frankie's
1990 concert in Cleveland. (Photo: Rita Rose)

Acknowledgments

This 18-month project would not have been possible without some very special people in my life. Many, many thanks to Jackie Musgrave, who edited and polished each chapter before I submitted them to the publisher; Nick Strange, whose photography expertise helped to enhance the photos in this book, and for designing this spectacular cover with one of his own rare photos of Annette; Lorraine Santoli, Disney publicist and author who put me in touch with the Mouseketeers; Arlene Ludwig, Disney publicist who generously kept my fan club supplied with Annette's photos and press kits (plus Disneyland passes!); Bonnie Wendt, who put me in touch with Annette in 1961 and has been a longtime friend; Bill Gerace, whose dogged persistence paid off in connecting me with Shelley Fabares; Janean Gilbert, who backed up my files on her computer and gave me encouragement; Lynn Hopper, a veteran journalist who has always believed in me; and Ann Ellerbrook, whose cheerleading and whip-cracking urged me along despite some frustrations. And, of course, my publisher and editor, Bob McLain at Theme Park Press, who made this labor of love possible.

Visit us on Facebook: Annette Funicello Tributes Book
Contact the author: RitaVRose46@gmail.com

About the Author

Rita Vandeveer Rose became an ardent fan of the *Mickey Mouse Club* in 1955 and started a national fan club for Annette in 1961. She is a retired Assistant Arts & Entertainment Editor and reporter for *The Indianapolis Star*, where she worked for 43 years. Currently, she is Executive Assistant to two independent TV shows, *Pet Pals TV* and *Great Day TV with Patty Spitler*, where she blogs on their websites and does a lot of dog-sitting. She has written one previous book, *World's Tallest Woman: The Giantess of Shelbyville High* (Hawthorne Publishing, 2008). Rita lives in Indianapolis with her cat, Spike.

Rita ran Annette's fan club for nearly
three decades and visited her often.
(1985 photo: Rita Rose Collection)

Rita Rose today. (Photo: Ed Stewart)

"Life doesn't have to be perfect to be wonderful."
—Annette Funicello

ABOUT THEME PARK PRESS

Theme Park Press publishes books primarily about the Disney company, its history, culture, films, animation, and theme parks, as well as theme parks in general.

Our authors include noted historians, animators, Imagineers, and experts in the theme park industry.

We also publish many books by first-time authors, with topics ranging from fiction to theme park guides.

And we're always looking for new talent. If you'd like to write for us, or if you're interested in the many other titles in our catalog, please visit:

www.ThemeParkPress.com

• •

Theme Park Press Newsletter

Subscribe to our free email newsletter and enjoy:

- ◆ Free book downloads and giveaways
- ◆ Access to excerpts from our many books
- ◆ Announcements of forthcoming releases
- ◆ Exclusive additional content and chapters
- ◆ And more good stuff available nowhere else

To subscribe, visit www.ThemeParkPress.com, or send email to newsletter@themeparkpress.com.

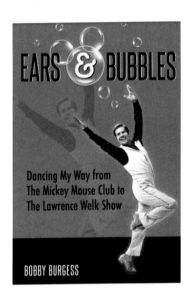

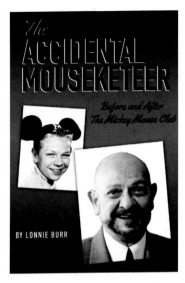

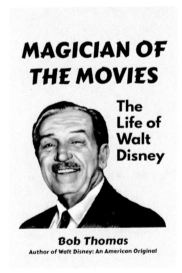

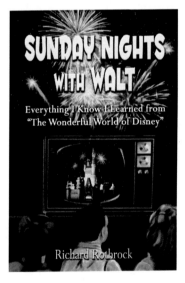

Read more about these books
and our many other titles at:

www.ThemeParkPress.com

Made in United States
North Haven, CT
20 March 2023

34312571R00087